"With the artful hand of a novelist and the soul of a healer, Trevor Carolan brings a quarter of a century of wisdom and experience to bear as he takes us on a colorful journey into the Tao of Tai Chi. Roaming from Vancouver's China-town to a gaudy Las Vegas hotel, 'playing' Tai Chi with Allen Ginsberg and finding poetry in a sword sequence, Carolan is the perfect guide to a world where 'the wind blows through the plum blossoms' and 'the fish leaps over the dragon gate.' It's a world where stillness comes from motion, teachers appear whether or not students are ready, and magic happens when you let go of effort. *Return to Stillness* is full of wisdom and insight. Anyone who plays Tai Chi will find lasting treasures in its pages."

—LEZA LOWITZ, poet and translator, author of
Yoga Poems: Lines to Unfold By

"At turns warm, elegant, instructive, mystical, and funny, this account of a devoted Western student of Tai Chi and his wise and venerated teacher will surely be a resource and inspiration to all those interested in not only the practice of Tai Chi, but the practice of whatever path of the heart they might follow."

—MIKE O'CONNOR, poet, and translator (with Steven R. Johnson) of
Where the World Does Not Follow: Buddhist China in Picture and Poem

"From ramshackle Chinatown café Vancouver to North Pacific snow peak, from edgy Las Vegas hotel to isolated Hawaii village, Trevor Carolan has written an exhilarating chronicle indeed. Here are useful forays into philosophies and poetries behind the art of Tai Chi and savvy accounts of its basis in the cycles of nature. Throughout the book Master Ng Ching-Por shows up in glimpses, 'hidden in hiddenness.' Then Carolan locates a North American totem, the great blue heron-and the ancient teacher reveals himself."

—ANDREW SCHELLING, author of *Wild Form, Savage Grammar*

"Trevor Carolan's prose embodies the calm of his subject. *Return to Stillness* is a testament to his commitment to achieving the grace that only comes through practice. Carolan is a keen observer, even of his own failures and triumphs. He finds the heart of each story and leaves us there to work out the implications. Like Tai Chi, his voice is steady, patient, and cumulative."

—REX WEYLER, author of *Blood of the Land* and *Song of the Whale* and co-author of *Chop Wood, Carry Water: A Guide to Finding Spiritual Fulfillment in Everyday Life*

RETURN TO
STILLNESS

Also by Trevor Carolan

Celtic Highway

Giving Up Poetry: With Allen Ginsberg at Hollyhock

The Colors of Heaven: Short Stories from the Pacific Rim (editor)

The Pillow Book of Dr. Jazz: Travels Along Asia's Dharma Trail

Translated by Trevor Carolan

The Supreme Way: Inner Teachings of the Southern Mountain Tao
(with Du Liang)

The Book of the Heart: Embracing the Tao
(with Bella Chen)

RETURN TO STILLNESS

STILLNESS

TWENTY YEARS WITH A TAI CHI MASTER

TREVOR CAROLAN

MARLOWE & COMPANY
NEW YORK

Published by
Marlowe & Company
An Imprint of Avalon Publishing Group Incorporated
161 William Street, 16th Floor
New York, NY 10038

Note: Cantonese terms throughout are rendered phonetically without
diacritical accent marks.

Page 237 represents a continuation of the copyright page.
Illustration on page viii © 2003 by Simon M. Sullivan

Library of Congress Cataloging-in-Publication Data

Carolan, Trevor
Return to Stillness : twenty years with a tai chi master / by Trevor Carolan.
p.cm.
Includes bibliographic references.
ISBN 1-56924-487-1
1. Tai chi--Philosophy. 2. Teacher-student relationships. I. Title.
GV504.C35 2003
613.7'148--dc21   2003042157

9 8 7 6 5 4 3 2 1

Interior design by Simon M. Sullivan
Printed in the United States of America
Distributed by Publishers Group West

For my teachers,
in gratitude

"The squeaking of the pump sounds as necessary as the music of the spheres."

—HENRY DAVID THOREAU

CONTENTS

INTRODUCTION

SOMEWHERE IN THE MISTS of early China, men and women first discovered the mystic dance of the heron and the snake, the dragon, tiger, and monkey. Over time, this nature wisdom evolved as a way of living gracefully and mindfully in the world—into the practice of Tai Chi—and people have followed it ever since, surely with good reason. Increasingly, as more and more people in the West seek to emulate this ancient discipline practice, they recognize it also becomes a path toward achieving balance in mind, body, and spirit.

I once asked my old master Ng Ching-Por—the *Sifu* of these tales—how we would recognize when we've finally arrived at the place we set out for with our practice of Tai Chi.

"How would we know when we'd really got it?"

Sifu's spartan English was always better than my awful Chinese. "Mr. Trevor," he said with his usual expression, something between placidity and a smile, "everybody must find own form.

I *Sifu*." At this he pointed to his breast. "No one can know my Tai Chi.

"*You* can be Sifu." He was staring at me now, emphatically, arms loose by his sides—this man who had become as dear to me as the grandfather I'd never had. "No one can know you-ar Tai Chi."

"That was Sifu," as my friend Fred insightfully remarked. "No magic slogans. At the end, it's simply your own being—each of us struggling to master our own form, striving to bond our hearts with the specific techniques that we learn from the teacher. Each of us has to find our own way, our own Tai Chi." My friend Fred is a financial comptroller, a Taoist economist in a job requiring sharp acuity of eye in balancing contending demands on material resources. He'd keyed in on one of the deepest truths our old teacher professed.

As the author of this work, I had been looking at the larger compass of the book much like an artist calculating if the canvas before him is sufficiently tempered in tone and color, rhythm and mood. Hearing Sifu's voice echoed in Fred Young's words, I was more than grateful for the reminder. It's like that with Tai Chi. When we find our teacher, even when they pass from this physical realm, their voice and spirit remain with us; and in those remarkable, ineffable moments when we are supremely blessed, we sense them moving within our own form, directing the movement and flow of *our* heron dance, precisely the way they articulated those same movements while still in physical form, and when as acolytes we followed beside them, or behind them, step-for-step in the mystery.

In compiling these stories from my twenty-three-year apprenticeship in Vancouver's Chinatown with the venerable Master Ng Ching-Por, I searched for incidents that would be most useful both to those new to the practice of Tai Chi, and to those already familiar with this ancient, traditionally secretive, Asian wisdom path. Typically, during my long years with Sifu, I was his sole Western student, and during the early years of my training especially, I struggled to grasp the deeper levels of meaning in Tai Chi practice and its Taoist philosophy that can be so perplexing to put into words in any language. Some things, Sifu taught, we can only comprehend with our heart.

The accounts that follow are gleaned from this Western seeker's cultivation and practice of Tai Chi Chuan kung fu. They are rooted in China's Southern Mountain Taoist tradition of natural science, meditation, and the martial and healing arts. Mostly, they were acquired through long hours of training with Master Ng, whom I met in the late 1970s shortly after his arrival in North America from Hong Kong, and with his small group of disciples.

Other than the traditional Chinese form in which I gained initiation through long experience and much laughter and aching bones, these modern Taoist tales make no claim on anyone's spiritual or temporal domain; nor is it their intent to weaken anyone's specific faith. In this regard, they can be viewed as complementary to contemporary interfaith dialogue, and where appropriate, they may create a bridge between Tai Chi practice and other spiritual traditions such as Buddhism and Judeo-Christianity. Shamanic principles simply come with the territory.

Throughout my apprenticeship with Sifu, his words and actions often reminded me of other instructors that I was occasionally privileged to hear through my work as a journalist: great dharma teachers like His Holiness the Dalai Lama, Thich Nhat Hanh, Robert Aitken-Roshi, and Kalu Rinpoche—all whose precious words have consistently urged a deeper relationship with one's heart, with compassion, and I bow to their wisdom.

Although readers will discover an abundance of information concerning the theory and mechanics of Tai Chi practice—beyond what has typically been available in English texts—this book is not offered specifically as a "how to" manual. No book can possibly replace the profound insights one receives from a fine teacher, and currently there are many good, and some not so good, teachers of the Taoist traditions available in the West. Rather, these passages constitute what the Japanese call "palm of the hand" tales, small epiphanies, or glimpses drawn from a Western seeker's everyday study of Taoism's Tai Chi path of grace and wonder.

As a practitioner of Tai Chi, who is also a journalist and university instructor of Asian philosophy, my intent is to provide the Western reader with a fresh and deeper understanding of *why, how,* and *in what spirit* a traditional Tai Chi master's movements are informed by this ancient wisdom path. As any truly serious student soon learns, Tai Chi represents a commitment, and once we begin the practice, it becomes what we ultimately never cease to do. It is a life's work, and to the casual onlooker it may appear relentless. Yet if one is genuinely involved with Tai Chi as a way of living more practically and simply, one is never too tired for regular practice. Indeed, as I was to discover, the practice of Tai Chi is something one begins to live, like a faith tradition, close to, or as an adjunct to, religion. Is it that serious? Well, only if we want it to be.

At some point in Tai Chi practice, if we're serious, we inevitably encounter the voice of stillness, and as Sifu Ng attempted to impart to his students, it is a difficult thing to describe. But when the chi is flowing, and the music of the spheres is in attunement, we experience the sacramental. For most of us in the Tai Chi realm, it is this that draws us back— because like sex and good business, when it's good, it's great; and when it's less than great, it's still pretty good. These stories are, by turn, anecdotal and sacramental, exemplifying the music of what happens when we adopt Tai Chi as an ongoing commitment.

Above all, it is my hope that you will find them relevant and practical to your own experience.

Offering specific insights into the challenges and blocks that invariably rise in our study of Tai Chi, each chapter also provides suggestions for overcoming these blocks. From experience, I've become aware that a typical frustration for newcomers to Tai Chi concerns the relative lack of written material addressing the fundamental dynamics of Asian teacher–student relationships. Asian traditions, for example, compel a deeper, more complex engagement with the teacher. It's not like dealing with the personable basketball coach from high school. Training in an Asian form of practice can become close like family, and tales of student exploitation are by now common enough that caveat emptor should apply in any such situation. But what about holiness? What happens when we come to regard our teacher as something close to a saint?

Read on, MacDuff.

Many neophytes are often too embarrassed and shy to pose questions that it seems everyone else in the room already has the answer to—like, "What happens, Sifu, when we die?" or questions about the mechanics of breathing, chi circulation and transmission, or whether Taoist and Buddhist meditation techniques are the same. How *does* one contend with the competitive urges that arise when one simply wants to be the apple of the teacher's eye, anointed as chosen dharma heir? How, even, does one deal with *Big Moment* awakenings or, more likely, their gawky absence? These are issues worthy of discussion. How often in the past I could have used such advice! Would it have spared me from repeatedly heaping hilarious embarrassment upon myself? I doubt it. Everybody pays his or her dues.

Readers will note that woven throughout this tapestry of anecdote and information is a significant element of nature-oriented dharma writing. As students gradually come to realize, when we relocate our practice to the world outside—a park, garden, or rooftop deck—it brings us closer to the organic cycles of the world around us. In paying close attention to our movement and breath, we naturally begin paying equal attention to the air we breathe, and the space in which we move. As a moving meditation exercise and martial drill, Tai Chi derives from Taoism, which begins and ends with the mystery of nature. So, let us observe it, and see what we really see. A treasured Zen riddle asks, "Why did Bodhidharma come from out of the West?" I've often wondered, "What brought Tai Chi *to* the West?" The answer in either case is always personal, necessarily involving a response similar to "In order to get us down to serious business."

These, then, are accounts about learning, playing, and ultimately bringing Tai Chi practice into our daily life from the inside out. In some sense, the book is also a conversation about inviting it out of the training hall, and incorporating its fuller harmony into our ongoing, everyday lives. As Sifu might have said, "Why else even bother?" In the end, those eager to learn the art and skill of Tai Chi will recognize the practical advantage of Sifu Ng's admonition that we all, in time, must master our own form. Those already on the path will understand that this process of self-actualization is ultimately based on learning: that before we are able to dissolve and break through all the tried and tested dharmas into something uniquely our own, we must first have persevered in mastering each critical step along the way. There are few, if any, sudden leaps into mastery. Need we be reminded that Tao—the spirit that breathes the primal chi—is a Chinese term for path, or "way"?

As my Tai Chi friend Fred enjoys explaining, everything that we ever learned from our old master's example essentially centers upon the Tao, and not so very much upon the "Tai Chi." For just as the original Taoist sage Lao-tzu has been whispering from the blossoms for twenty-five hundred years, it is the Tao that is the essence, and our Tai Chi merely its physical manifestations.

Without the essence—the embodiment of the Tao—our morning Tai Chi practice would not amount to much, and the meditative heron we spy along the shore would not speak to us of the return to stillness. Ideally, you will find this book worthy of your attention. If its merits are sufficient, you'll want to keep it handy and return to it when you feel the need. In whatever manner you choose to use and share it, as the H. H. the Dalai Lama suggests, the end goal is simple: health, wisdom, happiness, and the great jewel of compassion.

May you count the wise to be the wealthy, and may your Tai Chi practice be blessed.

Aloha,
Trevor Carolan

Hour of the Heron
Mount Seymour, British Columbia

1

FIRST INTIMATIONS

M Y INTRODUCTION TO TAI CHI came in the form of an apocryphal tale thirty years ago. After roaming late-sixties Europe and Asia for several years, I had returned to my West Coast hometown rich in experience. With only dead-end jobs available, I enrolled in a night-school anthropology course at a local college. The tutor, an unreconstructed, draft-dodging American hippie, effused wildly romantic notions of traditional Plains Indian culture. Fortunately, he encouraged students to pursue individual interests. India still fascinated me from my travels there, so while my classmates read Carlos Castenada's de rigueur exploits of the times, I explored the nature of Hindu culture.

Oral research presentations set the tone for our weekly seminar discussions. During my own tutorial, the instructor pulled fragrantly at his pipe while musing aloud on Native American approximations of the Brahmins' concept of Zero. Yoga, too, he added, had its plains aboriginal variants, as it did among the Chinese.

"A kind of Chinese yoga—Tai Chi it's called," he informed. "Elderly practitioners may take thirty minutes to move their arm from here to here," he said, gesturing a few inches with his forearm. The Castenada faction nodded knowingly. Shortly thereafter, a fashionable film about mate-swapping in California included brief footage of what appeared to be Tai Chi exercises.

A year later, having moved to California, I attended a concert ballet performance of *Swan Lake*. The program began with a flutter of crinolines. As lights and music dimmed, a strong lean male took center stage, moving slowly and elegantly, his swanlike poise exuding tranquillity. A soft, blue spotlight tracked his solo throughout, shadowing the grace and economy of his efforts. His presence was magically calming, and I sensed instinctively that what I was seeing was precisely what my life most needed at that point. Glancing at my program I noted his biography: Okinawa, Eurasian, Yang school of Tai Chi Chuan. After the show, I asked a friend to arrange an introduction.

The artist lived on a dairy farm in a neglected part of the local countryside, and I made my way there accordingly. It was a quiet afternoon and I called out my arrival. After a time, the man I recognized as the Tai Chi dancer presented himself. His working clothes were well soiled and he tromped up to say hello in muddy rubber boots.

We met and talked in the milking shed. The cows had not yet come in from the fields.

Our palaver was brief. I explained my purpose and asked, "Do you teach?"

"No," he replied single-mindedly. His tone was firm, but not unfriendly.

"Not at all? Could you teach me privately, here?" I ventured hopefully.

"I don't teach," he said. "I work with the dance group once or twice a year as a favor. That's all."

Two weeks later I returned again. "Sorry," he repeated.

There was nothing for it. That summer, I returned north to Vancouver and found work in a cemetery filling gravesites. The job couldn't have been quieter and was custom-made for daylong meditations on the transience of this physical world. Noontimes, I camped beneath a shady maple reading Kenneth Rexroth, Basho the wanderer, and Alan Watts. Then one morning, walking to work, I encountered a pair of visiting Brahmin priests from Kanpur, northern India, who said they were on a lecture visit to local Indo-communities.

Would I care to join them at their lecture that evening? they asked.

Next afternoon we went strolling together. Further to their lecture of the night before that I had attended, I asked, "Are there other ways to enlightenment other than by following a teacher?"

"*Guru* and *chela,* teacher and disciple—there is no other way," they declared.

I am not so sure that I was consciously seeking a teacher when an advertisement caught my eye a short time later, but a suburban high school announced that Tai Chi classes would be offered Monday nights. I ventured to take a look. Arriving at the gym, I saw a small group of women limbering up. Almost immediately, a cigarette-puffing Chinese instructor of about age fifty or so busied himself before me, discouraging my entry. "Too full, too full! No room!" he coughed with a sweep of his hand in my direction. His bandy-rooster coarseness caught me unprepared for the brush-off. Wrong place, wrong time, wrong teacher, I concluded.

Under the influence of Alan Watts's primer *The Spirit of Zen,* I'd begun a weekend study of Japanese *sumi-e,* black-ink painting. Kazu, my instructor, was a cheerful, selfless man who ran a small appliance repair shop on the city's ethnic eastside. Through his intervention, I was guided to another Tai Chi class due to start evenings at a nearby school slated for municipal demolition.

It was a rainy Tuesday and I arrived at an overcrowded classroom with desks piled up against the walls. An elderly Chinese gentleman who spoke no English led the class. Instead, his son-in-law served as interpreter to the forty-nine curious onlookers that had turned up to learn. My long apprenticeship began that night, a hopeless muddle at first, mitigated only slightly by the words of a woman I befriended who had been through it all before in Montreal.

"When everything else in life goes haywire, I've learned to drop out and just float a few times through 'Cloudy Hands,'"she said. Alas, within a few weeks she floated away impermanently herself, but her message was worth remembering.

Ng Ching-Por, the instructor, was a small, robust figure, seventy-five years of age, who moved like a man of forty. Most striking about his appearance was his hair—short for the times, almost shaved—and the unusual length of his eyebrows that curved dragonlike, outward away from his face. As an introduction, he performed three sets of Tai Chi. The classroom audience was a single hush at the astonishing beauty of the old man's movements, each one economical and efficient, and the suppleness of his hands magnetic—like wild rye weaving in the wind. Oddly, atop the small trim of his hair, several long strands had a way of wafting together whenever he turned or bobbed his head. They moved, I thought, exactly like the willowy quiff of the great blue heron.

"He's a tiny dragon," I explained to my companion later that night.

My progress was slow and frustrating, but steady. I practiced daily as instructed, and read the few books available in English on Tai Chi and Taoism. Happily, the incomparable American author and hedonist Henry Miller had helped popularize Lao-tzu's essential Taoist compendium, the *Tao Te Ching*. With that, and aided by Thomas Merton's little book on the eccentric Chuang-tzu, I cobbled together a small piece of the Tao and grew to love it.

Within ten weeks, the original forty-nine students had dissolved away to merely two of us. The term was ending and, slated for demolition, the school where we practiced was shortly to be bashed to smithereens. There would be no more classes. Out of gratitude, I gifted my instructor with a picture I had painted.

"You want to learn Tai Chi," the old man said, accepting the gift and speaking through his son-in-law. I was unsure of whether he was asking me a question or making a statement. "You can learn now. Come to my house. Don't worry—you don't pay money."

The three of us stood beneath a streetlamp in the parking lot. I'd had time to learn, even in the most rudimentary form, no more than half the basic movements of the Yang style. I wanted to know more.

"How long will it take to learn the whole Tai Chi?" I asked. The old man looked at me as this was translated back to him.

"Ten years."

Ten long years? Me, who'd never committed to a thing in my life? The old man looked me straight in the eyes, waiting. Nothing I'd ever seen was remotely as absorbing as what he knew and taught.

"I'll come," I said with boyish determination, only half understanding the winding road ahead.

WHAT IT'S ALL ABOUT

2

TAI CHI CHUAN" OR Grand Ultimate Fist kung fu, is by nature at once part sacred dance, part physical exercise, part meditation, and part combat training. A connected series of body movements derived from a repertoire of 119 rhythmic gymnastics, it originated with Taoist sages in northern China. Its creation is usually attributed to the contemplative monk Chang San-feng, who adapted, then linked, the characteristic movements of five principal animals: the white Mongolian Sarus crane, snake, tiger, monkey, and mythic dragon. These creatures lend their names and natures to many of the individual movements of Tai Chi's form and content.

Tai Chi is an expression of Taoist self-training. Emphasizing the belief in an inner energy—the *chi,* or life force—it seeks to establish an inner point of harmony through the balance of external bodily vigor and inner meditative strength. This is achieved through concentration upon a series of slow-moving, ballet-like movements. When developed as a regular practice, Tai

Chi serves to cultivate one's inner chi, gradually enhancing its circulation throughout the body's five major internal organs, through the limbs, and following a pattern coaxial to that visualized in hatha yoga, upward through the spinal column to the crown of the head. In time, the major organs are strengthened, the respiratory, circulatory, and reproductive systems are toned, and the mind is disciplined, thereby promoting health and longevity. If this sounds improbable, it may be valuable to note that in traditional Chinese culture, Tai Chi masters—those who teach the breaking of bones—have customarily served also as healers and bonesetters.

The goal of Tai Chi is to improve the health of one's mind and body. Its theories may seem simple, but the movements themselves—and the consciousness underlying the manner in which these movements are expressed—can take a lifetime to perfect. Tai Chi movements are soft, slow, and relaxing. They can be safely practiced by those of all ages, resulting in enhanced degrees of cardiovascular activity and lower levels of personal bodily stress. To achieve the fuller harmony of Tai Chi, one must be patient and willing to adapt to a path of daily practice. For some, this practice will evolve beyond mere conditioning to become a spiritual path as well.

Taoism, from which Tai Chi derives, is devoted to individual attunement with the larger world behind appearances—with immanence, the ineffable holiness of *What Is.* An infinitely adaptive phenomenon, it coexists easily and peaceably with other traditions. As a physical manifestation of Taoist practice, or "moving meditation," Tai Chi's complementary expressions of stretching and relaxing rely upon the utility of *wu-wei,* of using gentility and nonresistance instead of force and muscle to accomplish the desired end.

Through steady, mindful practice of Tai Chi, one can achieve health and longevity, as well as a general peace of mind from learning to apply Tai Chi's governing principles to daily life. For in learning to intuitively move both with, and away, from chaotic, hostile, or unpredictable currents of energy, we amplify our optimum responsiveness to such situations as they arise spontaneously in personal, family, and business life.

Tai Chi's methods of martial self-training promote enhanced confidence and self-reliance. Because long periods of study with a teacher are required to learn the minutiae of nuance and gesture incumbent in each Tai Chi posture and movement, patience and perseverance are also developed. And if one is sincere in wishing to advance his or her knowledge of the art, loyalty to both teacher and fellow students is essential. To these cardinal virtues one might further add the values of righteousness in dealing justly with others; frugality of human appetites; modesty and benevolence in relating to others in a kindly, courteous manner; humility; and integrity in holding faithfully to the truth of *Tao*—the grand Unity of all things under heaven.

Cumulatively, Tai Chi practitioners find these attributes to be a concrete way of dealing with the chronic restlessness, anxiety, and distraction of our contemporary culture. Through steady practice and application of Tai Chi's Taoist principle of maintaining inner balance not only within our exercise and meditation periods, but throughout our daily life activities—at work, at home, on the street, or while driving—we come to appreciate how Tai Chi offers a unifying, holistic approach to living mindfully in a world of change and impermanence. Like Zen, which itself derives originally from the mingling in China of Buddhism and Taoism, we strive to live our Tai Chi all the time. It is a singular approach, a path of subtlety, self-insight, and humor based on simply doing what needs to be done in the garden-variety business of living mindfully and happily on this precious planet.

3
THE DIVINITY GROOVE

S LOW TO TAKE UP Master Ng's offer of personal instruction at his home, I continued to practice alone what I had already learned with him. I also read whatever material presented itself on Tai Chi and other ancillary themes—mainly Buddhist.

An offer to travel came up unexpectedly and I found myself first in Toronto, then in New York on lengthy work assignments. Not knowing Toronto well, the only inner-city greenspace I found to practice in was the grounds of an old Roman Catholic church. Mornings, I repaired to a quiet corner of the churchyard and began moving beneath a leafy maple. Although no one disturbed me, a few robed clerics did give me quizzical looks. In gratitude, I began lighting votive candles at a small shrine before setting off back to my digs.

New York was a Dalí stew of people and emotions. I took trains to interview composers and musicians, returning each evening to the far Bronx where I bunked with family relations. One afternoon, while sitting in a midtown Manhattan bus, I was thankful for the self-defense training I'd received from Master Ng when it saved me from the worst of a frenzied stranger's angry swipe at the world. Next morning, working out in a local garden, I made a vow to complete my training when I returned to the West Coast.

But back in Vancouver, I was utterly unable to locate Master Ng. Unaccountably, I'd misplaced his address. Searching the phone book drew a blank. The school where he'd taught was a vacant lot heaped with rubble. What to do?

In a burst of enthusiasm, I headed for Chinatown, snooping around doorways, cruising side streets, inquiring in restaurants. No one could help me. Then one Saturday, I checked in again at a Chinese newspaper where a young journalist had previously tried to help me. Remembering my earlier enquiry, she'd made an effort to locate what few Tai Chi schools then existed. Following her directions, I set off in search of a storefront address deep in the waterfront tenderloin. I arrived at an open-door studio exactly in time to witness a burly Chinese instructor lift and project a lanky Canuck into orbit who finally crash-landed against an unforgiving wall. The shocked thump and swish of the astronaut's ponytail in flight was unforgettable. Then and there, I decided to take a rain check on the school of hard knocks, but not without filing away in memory the move that launched the ungainly student combatant.

A week later, I tried again at the newspaper. Perhaps there was news of Master Ng?

Unfortunately, not. Then might my lone contact recommend a decent place to eat while I persevered in my quest? That, the reporter could do happily. And in what evolved as a character-building exercise, I began eating regularly at Yick Fung, one of the last old Cantonese sojourner cafés on Chinatown's funky Pender Street.

The season passed into autumn, the rainy season. Pounding the city's downtown streets on my rounds in search of freelance assignments, I nipped often into Yick Fung. The grub was unbeatable: duck and dried bean-curd in soup, curried lamb stew noodles. Always cheap and scalding hot.

One steaming afternoon with monsoon rains pitching buckets outside, I barged in and took my regular booth. Fifteen minutes later, slurping hot broth, I noticed a pair of hands lower a newspaper two booths farther down. With a holler, I threw my arms wide for joy: Master Ng was beckoning me to join him.

We caught up on our news in spectacularly fractured English. Master Ng explained that since we last parted company he had established a school in Chinatown. Tuesday and Friday evenings he taught a small group of students in an old merchant block. Three nights later I was there. It looked like a movie set—the meeting hall of the Chinese Benevolent Association: framed portraits of Dr. Sun Yat-sen and Chiang Kai-shek above the stage, Chinese landscape scrolls around the walls, cramped offices, a reading room, kitchen, and cabinets full of antiquities. Gongs, lion-dance costumes, and the stringed instruments of the local Peking Opera orchestra jammed every nook. Nothing at all like a high-school classroom.

And so it began; five hours a week in Chinatown, half days on Sundays; an hour each morning at home—learning Tai Chi. The group of students that devoted themselves to Master Ng and his instruction called him *Sifu,* master. It was a name I liked. Wherever we might be—in a tea shop, an apothecary's, or walking the streets—someone would always approach with a near-invisible bow of the waist, and the title would spring forth: *Sifu.* As time passed, I saw that the meaning was archetypal; that the concept of a wisdom teacher extended throughout the Chinese community. The concept of mastery, it seemed, was a touchstone in itself, emblematic of three thousand years of East Asian evolution.

I observed in time that Sifu's teaching was always informal. In traditional Asian fashion, he taught by example. One-on-one, he would work with students through the evening, and it was in pure imitation of his movements that the heart of a session's practice was constituted. Repetition was everything: mind-numbing, bone-aching repetition. Always there was a core group of students; mainly, but not exclusively, young men like myself. Since the teaching was exclusively in Chinese, mimetic instruction had to work for me. One practiced individually or teamed up to make a pair, working on developing the intricate footwork that shapes the Tai Chi foundation. From this strengthened foundation one then explored the elegant handwork that characterized Master Ng's technique. Only by training and strengthening our point of contact with the ground, he taught, could we truly relax our whole upper body for optimum responsiveness in self-defense.

"*Fong sung, fong sung*," he repeated often: "Make it soft."

The only knack, as committed students came to learn, was to work through frustration whenever it arose.

We were fortunate in having Mah, an enviably talented senior student, to help Sifu with our instruction. Mah moved like a water spider. His ability, originally developed in Hong Kong, was a marvel. During the course of an evening he moved about the room, working with each student, demonstrating this or that aspect of Sifu's technique. Luckily for me, he was eager to learn English, and with his ESL worked hard to explain Sifu's commentaries. More by default than anything else, each week I also picked up a few Chinese words. It all helped, and as I stayed the course somehow things came together as a whole.

Late each evening, our group of six or seven lined up as Sifu led us mindfully through a full, long set. Each occasion, we added a little more new knowledge. What we didn't know, we faked—copying Sifu's movements as best as we were able. Indeed, by Western standards, there was little overt structure to Sifu's classes. You came and went at your own pace. "Sooner or later you'll get it," other regulars would say about some new tricky or difficult new maneuver. And always it was so. Newcomers like myself arrived from time to time and fit in as best as they could, making their own place within the family. Inasmuch as it was a Chinese school, an occasional Westerner or two would turn up, curious about receiving instruction, but the informality and otherness of the foreign environment proved difficult for most of them to grasp and they soon faded away.

Inevitably, in spiritual practice when our teacher is kindly and benevolent, we begin romanticizing their virtues. For a year or two I was no different, leaning toward hagiographic respect for my teacher. Even here, though, enlightenment necessarily unfolded.

Mah, Sifu's golden student who had come by his favor honorably through the dint of hard work, selflessness, and by making himself available to Sifu and his wife for many small tasks, had a problem. As a young man in a new country, increasingly he was compelled to direct his energies toward learning English for purposes of his working future. This was understood. Sifu himself had begun to study English each morning at a local college, and hoping to further bridge the language barrier, I had begun my own classes in Cantonese.

By and by, it became obvious that Mah was moving on to something else in his life. It was a painful realization shared by everyone in Sifu's group, for Mah's role had been considerably more than that of simple student and teaching assistant. What his larger role had precisely been was still unclear to me; certainly he dined a good deal with Sifu and his wife, Simo, on weekends.

As my own practice deepened, I'd taken to joining the three of them for dim sum every Sunday with my wife. From there, it naturally evolved into browsing and shopping together in Chinatown. Often, this led to an afternoon drive to some scenic place in the country with dinner following. As Mah's role became less prominent, that of my wife and me grew. As we spent more and more time with Sifu and Simo, the role became self-defining: I was heir apparent to Mah's long-held position of strolling companion and whatever else faithful students did within a traditional Chinese teacher–student relationship.

As our relationship developed, eventually we would help my teacher find an apartment, respond to government requests, and file documents and the like. Slowly, as my investment of time and emotion commitment grew, I came to appreciate what Mah had been to Sifu. I understood now how he'd crossed the threshold from student to disciple.

About this time, I wrote an article for a popular leisure magazine on the healthful benefits of Tai Chi, focusing the piece on Sifu. A television producer saw the feature and contacted Master Ng. Within a short time, courtesy of a television commercial sponsored by the Milk Producers Board, an elderly and very fit Chinese gentleman performing Tai Chi in a hilltop park backdropped by the rising sun brought millions of North American viewers coast to coast their first encounter with China's ancient heron dance. In the commercial's last sharp image, Sifu stood beaming, presenting a glass of fresh farm milk. North America had seen nothing like it before; public fascination was enormous and the Milk Board had itself a runaway success, spawning a host of copycat commercials over the years.

Sifu reported that he had been well compensated for the work and would continue to receive residual royalties. In the Chinese tradition, he threw a grand dinner to share his good fortune. My wife and I had often dined and been entertained by Sifu and Simo, but this would be different. My honorable teacher was hosting a celebration. With proper humility, my wife and I ventured forth.

It was a spectacular success, a gathering of Tai Chi people, assorted media types, and Sifu's own family. What I hadn't expected was the passion with which the Chinese invest such festive occasions. Bottles of costly XO Cognac mushroomed on the restaurant tables; the toasting was positively Arthurian. Sifu frolicked and jested like—well, like a very delighted human being.

Somehow I hadn't expected that. Did spiritual masters drink hard liquor? Only the very best of it apparently! My culturally imposed blinkers had suggested models of saints with stainless, ethical character. And here was my red-cheeked, precious teacher, sated after the fabulous meal he'd treated us all to, whooping it up and clearly tipsy. He reminded me of nothing so much as myself in the company of my dearest friends. But, never, surely, did spiritual masters like Sifu comport themselves like this, or did they?

Apparently, they did. We had a terrifically good time that night, marking a new plateau in our relationship. I'd learned that my teacher was human after all; he'd demonstrated that convincingly, perhaps even intentionally. The old divinity groove, I saw, brings as much constraint as it does enlightenment if we persist in allowing inauthentic or unrealistic expectations to govern our practice. Like confusing uncritical infatuation for love, I'd fallen for the sanctification rap.

"So what is real then?" we may find ourselves asking.

"Only relax," Sifu teaches. "Re-lax. . . . Inside must stay soft. Move from the heart."

"And our head, our mind?"

"Just don't think too much when you play Tai Chi. Don't you think! Only move, slowly."

This, disciples learn, is the real Tai Chi.

THE SPIRIT OF TAO

THE ORIGINS OF TAOISM began in the period preceding China's, and humanity's, first common era of settled village culture—in the approximately forty thousand years of undocumented human history we call the Neolithic. In China, as elsewhere, these origins root in the campfire personage of the tribal storyteller/lore-bearer: the shamanic seer.

China's native nature wisdom tradition led to the formulation of an oracle-bone system of spiritual divination during its Shang culture about 1700 B.C. Lore-bearers evolved a cosmology, or worldview, that in time would come to be known as the *Ba Gwa*—Taoism's often-seen "Eight Steps" symbolic of human and family structural relationships. These eight symbolic steps would come to be symbolized by the "Tai Chi," the "Great Principle" iconographic image interwoven from reciprocal male and female principles of primal polarity energies. Gradually, this system would define itself as a syllabus of knowledge, the *I Ching* that would harmonize shamanism's rough edges and provide human beings with instruction into the appropriate modes of action and conduct in particular situations.

Infused with the ideas of "Emptiness," or "Nothingness"— concepts that may have been introduced from Vedic Indian culture—China's evolving nature wisdom tradition would in time be identified with its governing precept, a concept explaining the panoply of everyday happenstance we know of as the world and its events: with *Tao*. Tao, or Way/Path, is the mystical Chinese visualization of that from which all things temporal and eternal emanate. Tao is the truth of *What Is.*

A path or "way," especially the Middle Way between extremes, Taoism is also known as "the watercourse way." As an approach to living that is natural, yielding, and effortless, Tao is an expression of the Great Watershed of creation, of the interdependent warp and weft of life that embraces both the chaos of precreation, and the primal harmony of Mother Nature.

Tempered by the concept of "duality," of male and female chi energies, Tao represents the necessary union of intuitive knowledge (yin) and cerebral, rational intelligence (yang).

Yin is associated with the darker, fecund, earth forces and is represented in Taoist inscription by three broken lines that are symbolic of "the well," or female sexual principle. Yang is associated with the fertilizing rain of heaven, and is represented by three unbroken rods, symbolic of the male principle.

Primarily, Taoism recognizes the interconnectedness between individuals and their surrounding environment. The point of balance that exists between the two is its central point of focus. As the daily practice of Tai Chi teaches par excellence, balance consists in the attunement of self with the subtly shifting energies of the larger world about us. Illness, for example, is seen as the inevitable consequence of slipping out of alignment with the cosmic flows and shifts of chi. Similarly, health results from the dynamic balance of the physical, psychological, and social components of our individual relationship with the larger world. Taoism's cultural worldview, then, can be seen as a weather-report equation in which physical, mental, and spiritual values are balanced alongside organizational, administrative, and economic principles.

Do Taoism's philosophical perspectives have application to the larger, modern world? It is a natural question. In his *Uncommon Wisdom,* Fritjof Capra, the distinguished Berkeley physicist and author of *The Tao of Physics,* addresses this issue while discussing the economist E. F. Schumacher—himself author of the path-breaking *Small Is Beautiful*—observing, "Societies need stability and change, order and freedom, tradition and innovation, planning and laissez-faire."

In short, both the yin and yang of existence.

As the philosophical underpinning of Tai Chi Chuan, Taoism

recognizes that our health and happiness depend on dualities, on the simultaneous pursuit of opposite activities and aims— on what poet Allen Ginsberg liked to call "the unity of dissimilars"; for example, Yeats's image of the "murderous innocence of the sea."

Unlike Confucianism, which sets forth a moral path in offering structure to society, and which may be viewed as being external in its application, Taoism presents a vision of natural order that is purely personal and internal. Taoism is wholistic and cyclical in concept. As Lao-tzu notes in his quintessential compendium of Taoist poems/texts, the *Tao Te Ching:*

> *Humanity follows earth*
> *Earth follows heaven*
> *Heaven follows Tao*
> *Tao follows what is Natural.*
> —#25 (translated by Gia-Fu Feng and Jane English)

Taoism regards nature as the ultimate teacher, emphasizing observation of the passing of seasons through mindful practice— the cultivation of mental and physical health through meditation, physical training exercises, the arts, and so on. Its "wisdom" consists of pragmatic, observable truths—although these truths may be intuitive by nature.

Taoism clarifies the belief in the essential oneness of the "ten thousand things," the image used by Taoists to describe the vastness of objective reality. In this way, it may be seen as pantheistic, but this should rightly be interpreted more as recognizing the "Godhead *in* all things," not "the God of each thing." In this, Taoism harks continually to that particular form of human understanding handed down from pre- and early Neolithic cultural evolution best intuited as the wisdom of the heart.

Original Taoist cosmology begins with recognition of the Great Void, the primal Emptiness or "pre-reflective" consciousness. In the wonderful collection of anecdotes that bears his name, Chuang-tzu, the second of Taoism's great saints, understands this consciousness as the *chi wu lun*—the fundamental unity and equality of all things. From this great spaciousness derives the essential Chi polarity priciple. And from this principle flow the twin, swirling polar energies of yin and yang. Here, *chi* can be read as meaning energy, cosmic energy in the same fashion as that envisioned by Yoga's *prajna* energy. Yet, at best, this is only an approximation, for in the Taoist context chi represents not so much a thing or an actual element, but a *process*—an ineluctable system of cyclical energy flows.

In the beginning, and extending into the eternal present moment, the primal energies swirl within the great void and are defined by the polarities of yin and yang. Unceasingly, these energies flow, waxing and waning respectively after the example of the moon. From their transformations arise Taoism's "ten thousand things": all the phenomena of the natural world. In *The Turning Point,* Fritjof Capra notes in a quote from the *I Ching:*

> *After a time of decay comes the turning point.*
> *The powerful light that has been banished returns.*
> *There is movement, but it is not brought about by*
> *Force. . . . This movement is natural, arising*
>   *spontaneously.*
> *For this reason the transformation of the old becomes easy.*

Becoming attuned to the transformational patterns of the Great Watershed of creation is not something that can be acquired from books. True Taoist practice is experiential and, traditionally, studied under the guidance of a master in one or another of the classic disciplines, Tai Chi among them. This teacher-student relationship is archetypal—instilling a sense of order, ritual, and self-discipline. The ideal of the accomplished master—the *Sifu,* or what might translate more recognizably as *Guru*—is central to Chinese civilization. It is he or she who performs the role of sage, shaping and guiding successive generations in the knowledge of responsible leadership, and expounding the virtues of justice, fairness, modesty, frugality, and self-discipline. As Loy Ching-Yuen, a modern Taoist master and the teacher of Sifu Ng, relates in his work *The Supreme Way:*

> *The mindful path, whatever its philosophical origin, offers the possibility of higher levels of self-awareness. Accordingly, we must be attentive in correcting our individual faults and mindful of our responsibilities to the world and to others. Is this not enlightenment of a kind?*

Taoism relies upon the joint foundation stones of modesty of nature—knowing when enough is enough; and self-attunement with nature—with what Pythagoras in earlier Western times called "the Music of the Spheres." Contemporary manifestations of Taoism remain equally vivid and can be recognized and understood through *Deep Ecology's* concept of living lightly and responsibly in stewardship with the earth. Or as Christendom once understood, *Ora et Labora:* our prayer and work are One.

As a practical philosophic-spiritual tradition, Taoism comes to us chiefly through the works of Lao-tzu, a librarian at the old capital of Loyang circa 500–450 B.C. Legend has it that upon retiring from the world, Lao-tzu left his eighty-one brief *pensées* with the imperial keeper of a mountain pass leading to the higher heights. His little book, the *Tao Te Ching,* is acknowledged as the

Taoist bible. Its amazingly spare dialogue provides epistles relating to: unity (#1), duality (#2), the essence of the Watercourse Way (#8), emptiness (#11), dealing with money and fame (#12), presentness/mindfulness (#14), veneration of the old and weathered/the mystery of the "uncarved block" (#15), moderation (#46), and other seminal Taoist values.

Henry Miller, who worked tirelessly to introduce intercultural perspectives into what he felt was the aridity of North American life, claimed the *Tao Te Ching* was the greatest book he'd ever read. Its gentle power soothes like a balm. Nowadays there are many good translations available and a tiny pocket companion traveler's edition helps you ensure that the inspirational genesis of the Taoist spirit remains portable on your journey through the world.

5

UNDERSTANDING CHI

S IFU NG IS FOND of explaining the importance of regular daily Tai Chi practice this way: "Playing Tai Chi is like putting money in the bank. We invest in our own healthy circulation of chi and can draw interest off it through the rest of the day."

With the rise of empirical, "provable" knowledge in Europe's seventeenth century, the four elements—earth, air, fire, and water—previously recognized by Aristotle as the essential components of Western medical and alchemical knowledge, gradually retreated from popular consciousness. From Shakespeare's time when it was understood as "ether," or as an integral element enjoining heaven, earth, and humanity in a primal trinity, chi has devolved in rational Western imagination to where it is now likely to be interpreted as a rather nebulous concept for "cosmic" energy.

We can imagine chi, however, as something like a primal vapor, the invisible white of an egg in which physical forms live and function, breathing in the chi that surrounds and nourishes them. Although a thousand years ago during the Sung dynasty, Chinese philosophers might have claimed that chi condenses like water and thus can be seen, in reality chi cannot be detected by the five senses. Rather, it is intuited through the process of stilling the mind to such a point that our awareness is invoked to a larger Oneness and vitality. Chi, then, is a quintessence.

As such, whatever exists and has mana—what the Polynesian peoples know as spiritual power—possesses chi. Tai Chi Chuan is the cultivation of this grand power through the practice of spiritual boxing. What we are doing in our physical exercise and moving meditation is no less than attuning ourselves to the mysterious energy of the divine.

In a similar fashion, the traditional aim of Chinese visual artists, poets, and calligraphers is to also forge links between their creative works and the Great Tao. Indeed, historically, the roles of the scholar, calligrapher, poet, and artist were singular. To become a master was to have achieved mastery in all four forms since each shared a commonality of materials—ink, brush, paper, and stone. In approximately A.D. 500, the principles of Chinese artwork were laid down by Hsieh Ho in his "Six Canons of Painting." First among these is that primary importance be given to the painterly expression of chi, of "impression resonance," thereby reaffirming the unbreakable bonds linking creativity with the eternal processes of Nature.

Practitioners of Tai Chi often speak of "moving the chi," of getting things going and toning up their bodily processes. To suffer illness or injury suggests being out of sync either physically, emotionally, or socially with the larger world. The health concerns of Tai Chi people promote a fair amount of touching and physical observation among them; hence it is not unusual to hear remarks such as "Her chi is weak" when discussing an ailing group member. Wounds, bone injury, or deep bruises are viewed as blockages to the free circulation of one's chi, and are therefore treated with medicinal care such as herbal infusions, topical poultices, or massage and acupressure to "open up the flow" of chi through an injured area.

In higher forms of Tai Chi practice this latter tradition is developed to a rarefied skill and constitutes the often-discussed, but much misunderstood, branch of Chinese healing popularly called *Chi Kung* (Qigong), which to the initiated is rightly known as *Nei Kung Yang Chi*. Acupuncturists, for example, develop extensive charts detailing the body's energy meridians. With the stimulation of certain points along these flow lines (which may mirror nerve or vascular systems), the bodily healing process—the flow of chi—can be initiated, or even abruptly kick-started in case of urgent situations where Western medicine may have little better to offer. Interestingly, martial artists have their own similar charts, and overlays of these reveal sophisticated levels of comparative knowledge. "To stop one's chi" is a Chinese way of expressing death, and in the darker martial shades of Tai Chi practice there exists a tradition of *dim mak,* or death-point striking technique.

Contrawise, we can cultivate and develop our chi. Much of this, of course, is plain common sense: eating, drinking, and sleeping correctly, right livelihood, right thinking, and so forth. And as Tai Chi practitioners we have an amazingly efficacious form of exercise therapy at our disposal.

Once our heart speaks to us and we learn to recognize this as the true voice of the Tao, the manifold layers of Tai Chi practice begin to reveal themselves and our skill grows in utilizing chi as an active principle within daily life—like a guardian energy source hidden in a secret pocket.

6

MAKING IT SOFT

S UNDAY MORNINGS I DRIVE to Sifu's place at eight o'clock.
I've done this for a long time, so I suppose in some ways it's like going to church. Occasionally, rain, frost, bitter cold, or snow gets in the way, but we carry on regardless.

We practice our Tai Chi at the school yard near where Sifu lived when he first arrived in North America. Our practice area is a basic asphalt courtyard covered with line markings for hop-scotch, roundball, what have you. If the weather gets bad, we can work in a covered shelter out of the rain. It's a good spot to have, and as there are always other groups roving about looking for such a site, keeping regular weekend hours there is essential in securing the space for our own sessions. We've been there for more than twenty years now.

Just as endurance earns its own respect, practicing out of doors is its own reward. The spacious playground attracts birdlife and surrounding trees are often bright with song. Vancouver is ringed to the north and east by a range of young, steep mountain peaks that remain snow-covered most of the year, offering a splendid view. Occasionally, broad-winged bald eagles soar overhead, and great blue herons heave across the sky toward their big-tree nests near the river.

Practicing outside, one notices the wash of the seasons; the pink buds that develop in late winter; the incremental lengthening or depletion of daylight; the changing angle of the sun or the shift of the tides. Above all, one becomes aware of Tai Chi as a nature-based wisdom path. Whether alone weekday mornings in our own neighborhoods, or as a group on weekends, outdoor practice is the root of our Tai Chi training.

There is something truly admirable in the deep, meditative quiet of mature adults silently practicing together of a morning. We begin with flexed-knee exercises from our horse-riding stance, raising our arms to third-eye/forehead height with soft, alternate shifts of the waist. This is the basic Tai Chi warm-up, good for soothing out morning backaches and developing stance and arm work. We rock our arms forward and backward in a steady rhythm, and add variations, stepping back on either the right or left foot to bear our full body weight as we continue weaving our arms upward. This is a demanding exercise: training the upward sweep and flex of our arms develops the raised hands blocking-work of Tai Chi's fundamental self-defense strategy. Whether in the "double-weighted" stance balancing on both feet, or in the single-weight stance on either left or right foot, we continue our arm sweeps while holding to our basic Tai Chi shadow-boxing posture.

Repulse the Monkey is a useful variant. From the horse stance we again flex knees, check our abdominal posture, and raise hands up. With elbows pointing to the ground we softly crook our forearms downward to a point about twelve inches in front of our sternum, and roughly horizontal to the ground. Using steady turns of the waist, we alternate the brush of our arms, flexing downward and softly raising the arms back up to starting position while avoiding the use of muscle.

The trick of Repulsing the Monkey is to imagine that the downward sweep of the hand and forearm is actually kneading a large ball of dough. Each hand ultimately aims for the same destination point—again centered some twelve inches from the sternum. Add a slight turn of the wrist when sweeping the hands back upward, and voilà!—a useful, repetitive training exercise that prepares one for the real-life self-defense function of backing out of unfavorable situations. The exercise can also, and ideally should, be conducted using a single-foot stance as well.

A third simple exercise is the Big Circle. From the horse stance again, the hands are raised in readiness position eight to ten inches from the body, elbows down. The idea is to rotate the waist in a circular motion. As the trunk of the body moves, shoulders and arms move too—all of the same motion. To complete the Big Circle, as we move clockwise to the left, we rotate our arms up from the shoulder, then rotate them down to the right and vice versa. As we swing to the left, we flex our knees upward slightly, lowering them as we reach the right-hand turn, and vice versa. The key is leaving the limbs and hips soft and fluid while repeatedly tracing a circle in midair with the hands. As the torso lifts, circles, and falls you will notice a certain abdominal crunch: this is also Tai Chi's most effective waistline reduction exercise. A ten-to fifteen-minute stretching regime of this type prepares anyone to play Tai Chi.

7

MOVING ZEN

I T FEELS GOOD TO play Tai Chi; that's why, in Chinese, people say *play* Tai Chi. Western students seem to get hung up grammatically on this, although in English they have no difficulty with the concept of "playing" the piano or playing video games. Because Tai Chi feels so good, and because it's so good for us, the extra effort to get things right is worth it.

Since Tai Chi is both ancient and foreign, among the first questions a newcomer asks is, "How should I breathe?" It's the perfect question, really. Within the answer lies the whole world of Taoist logic underpinning Tai Chi Chuan.

Sifu Ng always teaches that there is no secret decoder ring to breathing technique. The correct approach is to simply let our lungs tell us when and how to breathe. Tai Chi's softness can be deceptive. Its movements require dexterity and balance and even a fifteen-minute session leaves one with the awareness that physical exertion has taken place. Like water, breathing finds its own level. When the Yang style's more complicated sequences of movements leave one breathing heavier, they are always followed by connective gestures such as *Cloudy Hands* or the *Single Whip*. Their calm, flowing execution affords one the opportunity to make any breathing adjustments that may be necessary. The trick is to keep one's head out of it altogether.

Timing our individual Tai Chi movements is a related matter. As students, it is our role to emulate the model set by our teacher and, with sufficient practice in each other's company, no stopwatch will be needed to pace our own solo action elsewhere. Learning Tai Chi is a case of imprint-patterning. We do what our teacher does, and in time, what we do on our own becomes a close approximation of our teacher's model. Not perfectly identical, but close. As for the interior timing of our separate movements, like poetry they relate to our breath.

Playing Tai Chi—expressing each separate movement such as *Golden Phoenix* or *Repulse the Monkey*—is much the same as reading poetry aloud. The length of each expressive measure is aligned with our breath. Lines of poetry end when the breath expires and begin with inspiration. Similarly, if we commence movement simultaneously with the in-breath, the result is instantly apparent. Of course, not every breath or every movement will accord exactly with its counterpart, but successful Tai Chi practice develops through consistency in achieving unified performance. In moving with the chi, breath and movement, mind and body are one.

With breath and timing, stance is preeminent in helping develop the soft, flowing movements so characteristic of Tai Chi. Sifu notes that it is always Tai Chi's handwork and synchronized weaving of the arms that attracts onlookers to a skillful practitioner, while good footwork normally goes unnoticed. The important element in developing both footwork and supple upper-body movement is stance—which translates from Chinese as "sit-leg."

"Sit-leg" means to hold the body weight on one leg only. In bending our leg at the knee so that it is roughly in vertical line with the point of the toes, we are obliged to carry this weight with our shin, calf, and thigh. As outlined in the chapter "Closing the Gates: Tai Chi as Self-Defense," as our overall proficiency develops, we learn more advanced methods of shaping and carrying our body mass. Sit-leg is the heart of our stance-making ability, however, and requires lengthy training. One of the signs of advanced skill in the martial arts is the degree of proximity to the earth with which one can comport oneself in action—"how low can you go?" Achieving power in the sit-leg stance is not for everyone, nor is it purposed as such. Aging students, or those interested in Tai Chi as a light and healthful meditative pastime, are under no obligation in this area. Under no circumstances should anyone feel, or be made to feel, pressured into forcing this difficult training onto themselves. Like marathon zazen sesshins, sit-leg training can become very trying on the knees. The solution in such cases is to practice comfortably.

Whatever it is that we are seeking in Tai Chi, the key to achieving it is always through patience. Right Practice means steady, mindful daily practice, time after time, heartbeat after heartbeat. Frustration is inherent in our practice and only overcome through repetition and correct instruction. There is nothing in the Tai Chi corpus of knowledge that cannot be achieved through practice and patience, and this can sometimes be a considerable jolt. Practicing Tai Chi, it is natural for us to attempt to further our skills. In the beginning, we generally work from rough forms. Our teacher points the way and we follow as best we can. Picking up and memorizing the basic 108-form Yang style requires about three months, after which we begin polishing our execution, balance, and foot- and handwork. With time, as we are introduced to new techniques or better, sharper ways of expressing these techniques, we begin new phases of learning.

As our level of Tai Chi skill increases, it may seem that our actual rate of progress begins to slow down. This is natural. Our initial three-month learning period is a relative gush of acquiring a basic, pedestrian knowledge of an extremely evolved body of lore. Honing our understanding and expression of this raw block will constitute a lifetime of study, however, if we are prepared to dedicate ourselves. What we receive in our first three months or so is only the basic Tai Chi repertoire of movements; what follows during the next many years is the *kung fu* of this practice—the root wisdom of Taoism's Tai Chi dharma.

In Tai Chi practice, hitting plateaus of accomplishment where our progress seemed slow and hoping to break through to higher levels comes with the territory. Ironically, learning to recognize when we are treading water in a specific level of achievement seems to be part of finally breaking out of it. When we are introduced to a new form, the cutting technique of *Li* for example—one of the "four pillars" of Tai Chi self-defense—the model may seem perfectly clear. How we execute this technique—the turning of the waist; sit-leg stance; shaping of body, elbows, and shoulders all prior to, and part of, the actual cut itself—can be exasperating. We try it for weeks and then for a month without success. Our instructor and other students may help, yet we remain stumped, beached on a plateau until suddenly, mysteriously unbidden, it comes. Whatever was our problem? And for days thereafter, we experience the delight and wonder of *knowing*.

And so it goes. On to the next plateau.

8

WHAT IT'S **REALLY** ALL ABOUT

FOR YEARS, MY FELLOW students in Sifu's group suggested that one day I ought to write a book about Master Ng's approach to Tai Chi life. Ironically, when they learned I had begun keeping a journal on this subject, they were at a loss—as if I were about to give away the family secrets. Attempting to reassure them, I remembered Sifu's often-heard words that in the circumstances seemed especially apropos: What can one really say in words about Tai Chi anyway?

Once Mah had drifted away, Douglas Lau became Sifu's senior North American Chinese student. Both he and I began studying with Master Ng within a month or two of each other, but by dint of both a profound native cultural sensibility regarding the subject, and his ability to communicate and absorb Sifu's knowledge firsthand, he enjoyed the designation of *Si-heng,* elder student. As a term, it is almost never used, but signifies recognition among other students that the Si-heng is so much the nearer that final bit of achievement than the rest of us. General ranking in the "internal," or softer, schools of the martial arts is by seniority; everyone is more or less Si-heng to somebody else.

Newcomers must strive hard.

In sparring "push-hands" with an adept like Doug, one braces for another level of skill altogether. The practice of full-minded attention springs forward with the first lotus touch of his wrists. It had better—one only learns the hard way after being tossed off-balance scores of times. Doug and I stood talking together out of the wind on a raw November morning. After an hour or two of practice, other students had left for home, or repaired to restaurants for the Sunday ritual of dining together. "Writing a book is good," Doug said. "But you have to be careful about what you say. Like Sifu always tells us: You can learn only so much from books. At a certain point, you must experience it for yourself.

"This means it is very important to be clear about what we can promise to people who read such a book," he continued. "But that's your job: to make it so the English-speaking people can understand what is the real Tai Chi, and how we can learn the inside Tai Chi for our own best use."

This was as good a starting point for a book as any, I reckoned. It was from here that I began elaborating to Doug what I believed, and had been taught, was the most useful information for those either new to the art, or ongoing practitioners. As Doug extended his discourse in reply, I listened attentively.

"What we want to do is be healthy," he explained, echoing Sifu Ng. "We want to be healthy, that's all. This is why we play the Tai Chi—so that we can work ten hours without getting tired, or get headaches and a sore back. So that we can support our family.

"This is the real inside Chi Kung," he continued, and in his words I heard the resonant voice of old Master Ng. "Nowadays everybody talks about Chi Kung—it's like this; it's like that. . . . But real *inside* Chi Kung means learning how to relax and open ourselves up; purifying our mind so that we can take in more chi, to be peaceful and calm and live a long time with a good life."

Doug was talking about the deep stuff. I thought back to a summer gathering I'd attended where a well-known public television journalist, new to the city, remarked on his fascination with the Chinese practicing Tai Chi mornings in the park near his home. "Why do you do it?" he'd asked. "What's in it for you? Can you work up a sweat? It doesn't seem like a younger man's game."

Fair questions. In answering, I'd said something like, "Why do we practice? Well, to attain grace."

We chatted a while longer and I suspect he longed for a more complex response than what I'd offered. But I reminded myself that he might simply be sizing up the idea for an "infotainment" feature, rather than inquiring out of personal interest.

To be peaceful and calm. To live a long time with a good life, possibly attaining a little grace en route. Now there's your answer. That's the real secret according to Si-heng Doug. That's why we play Tai Chi Chuan.

9

WILD MEDICINE

I T's GOOD TO HAVE a talisman, a protective charm. Even technically nontheistic Tibetan Buddhists are given to hollering *Lha gyalo!* in thanks—Victory to the Gods!

Tai Chi offers us its own dharma guardians, notably the five animal spirits—heron, dragon, monkey, tiger, snake—that provide it with inspiration. All are beautiful and endowed with particular powers. Most Tai Chi people have their own favorite. When possible, it's beneficial to spend time around your inspiring animal, even if only at a game park. Short of sighting a bear or cougar in the wild, there is nothing like the frisson of studying a panther from reasonably up close to bring real focus to our execution of *Raise Hands and Slap the Face* or *Ride the Tiger.*

In the West, the crane or heron is the likeliest of the five animals we might see in the wild. Heron study is all about patience and admiration: a study in balance, poise, patience, coolness, and sudden attack. Wild cranes and herons are breathtaking, and through the years I've spent innumerable hours in their presence—in what Hindus call taking *darshan:* basking in the light of a holiness. Playing Tai Chi, I strive to bring what I've absorbed from the heron to my practice.

I met a *karateka,* a karate man, once at the beach. At various times, we'd seen each working out along a rocky, untamed stretch of shoreline. Tall, fit, and lean, in his kata sequences he struck low and fast, his kicks snapping straight and sharp from the knee. He knew what he was about, that was certain. Avoiding any competitive situation, we left each other alone and kept our peace.

One summer morning, we were introduced to each other by a mutual acquaintance. Soon, we found ourselves alone, our talk turning naturally enough to our respective forms of practice: the one, Japanese; the other, from China.

"It derives from heron-watching, Tai Chi," I said. "The way they spread, then fold their wings, swooping them in defensive circles, closing the doors, striking at snakes." I offered a small demonstration.

The karateka nodded. "Mine's the eagle," he said. "I saw one out by the lighthouse early this morning." He pointed left across the tidal flats.

"You should have seen him; he came from way out in the gulf," said the karateka, tracing the eagle's line of flight with his outstretched arm and fingertips. "He swooped the thermals near the cliffs there, and passed directly overhead toward the Indian reserve to the south. Then he headed for the forest and vanished."

As the other man spoke, I'd observed how the sweep of his arm sketched a perfect half-circle, all 180 degrees. Perhaps his waist had swiveled a little as he rotated left to right, but I did not see it. Then his hand swept softly down to near his thigh. His control and execution were flawless.

"Eagle medicine," I said with respect.

"Just karate," he responded, smiling. We reached out and shook; his grip was solid, unaffected.

We set off walking together. "Eagle medicine," he repeated warmly, trying it out.

"Sounds good. Worth cultivating." I nodded in agreement. There was nothing more to say.

With the merest shadow of a bow, and with our eyes still trained in respectful but friendly manner upon each other, we turned and made our way up a rugged escarpment trail that marked the return to civilization. The sound of the dharma hummed in my ear like wild medicine.

10

KOWLOON SLEIGHT OF HAND

ONE HOT SUMMER EVENING at the B.C. Royal Cafe—for years the only place in Chinatown you could get a cup of coffee after dark—Sifu told us a story from his Hong Kong days.

The incident took place in Kowloon Park on Nathan Road near the jewelers' district of Tsim Sha Shui and the East Indian cloth merchants, not far from the Star Ferry depot. At the time, Sifu worked as a watchmaker nearby, a trade he practiced after having fled the communists in Hangzhou.

Each morning in the park, Sifu played Tai Chi, pushing hands for an hour or so with a friend he'd known for twenty years. Afterward, the sparring partners repaired to a tea shop where they took breakfast before walking on to work. This particular occasion, however, two men approached Sifu in the park. The first was a businessman with whom he was slightly acquainted. Escorting him was a renowned teacher of *Hung Gar,* the powerful Tiger boxing style from Tibet.

The first man asked if Sifu would kindly demonstrate his style and form for the pair since they had heard much about him.

Often, such occasions are fraught with the risk of uncalled-for competitive behavior, or outbursts of one type or another. And so Sifu politely declined, suggesting that his talents hardly warranted attention. The honored visitor might visibly observe his form; however, it was likely he might find it wanting, or see nothing in it of consequence from his observation.

The Hung Gar man appeared either not to understand, or chose to reject Sifu's explanation. Instead, he requested aggressively that Sifu demonstrate his form and technique, allowing how he'd made a journey of considerable distance to witness exactly this thing. It had been spoken of highly, perhaps even possibly akin to his own long-studied mastery of the Hung Gar tradition.

There was no polite exit. The inevitable martial protocol was implicit. Some sort of match must follow such a physical demonstration.

Nevertheless, Sifu stood off and positioned himself loosely in his beginning flex-knee stance, standing and wavering slightly for some time with his eyes partly closed. Then, as Sifu explained it, in his mind's eye he embarked on deep movement through the first several sequences of Yang-style Tai Chi Chuan. Sinking further into stillness, he progressed onward through the set, using what is called the "internal" movement of one's chi energy.

Time passed. Concluding this silent, motionless exercise—Sifu had simply stood there quietly, more or less detached throughout—he turned to the visitors who had importuned him, and leaving forthwith with a friendly smile asked, "Okay, have to go now! Did you get it?"

With that, he took cordial leave with his friend. The two newcomers continued staring blankly at Sifu as if he were crazy.

"What?" the Hung Gar man blurted out as Sifu walked off to morning tea. "Why, I . . . I never saw a thing!"

11

CLOSING THE GATES:
TAI CHI AS SELF-DEFENSE

I N TAI CHI TERMS, the greatest defense is not having to defend at all. As Sifu Ng teaches every newcomer, "Your feet are your first, best option in a fight. Run!" Experience shows that many times oratory is even better, but it may pass that self-defense becomes unavoidable. For this reason, and because injustice must inevitably be dealt with, the individual movements of Tai Chi—apart from their meditative/regenerative functions—offer a practical means of dispatching aggression directed toward us.

Tai Chi is one of the three "internal" or soft schools in the Chinese martial arts. Ba Gwa, a walking form based on the power of the circle, and *Hsing I,* a northern style based on animal movements with a rise and fall in its rhythms, complete the trio. The three are popularly associated with Taoist monastic tradition in the Wudang Mountain area.

These Wudang traditions were established as Taoist alternatives to the diamond-hard, rapid-fire martial arts of the Shaolin mountain temple school founded by Bodhidharma, the Indian monk who brought Dhyana, or Chan (Zen in Japanese) Buddhism to China. Taoists viewed the aggressiveness of the Shaolin school—the form popularized through Bruce Lee–style kung fu films—as a technique that, while superb in its fighting character, undesirably propelled one's inner chi outward from the body. For this reason, the many schools of hard-style fighting arts descending from the Shaolin original are known as "external" forms.

His Holiness the Dalai Lama is fond of reminding us that as newcomers to an idea with which we identify, it is natural for us to distinguish it in some way, often by comparing or distancing it from other models. Tai Chi is no exception. While the internal systems have their own great advantages, there are drawbacks. Ordinarily, it takes a long time to become proficient in their practical use. By contrast, the external schools offer significantly advanced levels of martial ability in a much shorter period, yet they too have hindrances—frequency of injury and so forth. Both styles are equally valuable, and both are founded upon sound, healthful, meditative traditions. In their higher levels, both are equally superior in the promotion of healing, and in their martial applications. Ultimately, they are roads toward the same end. They are simply different in inspiration and expression.

Application of Tai Chi as a means of self-defense is based upon the Tai Chi circle with its eight nuclear "trigrams." These three-line representations correspond with the cardinal points of the circular compass (N, S, E, W), and the supplementary points (NE, NW, SE, SW). In addition, the "eight steps" direct our concentration of energy as we move; just as important, they help guide our footwork and concentration. Tai Chi self-defense relies on a series of movements, postures, and attitudes. Primarily, it is truly a "defense." Tai Chi follows the wu-wei principle of nonresistance and is essentially nonaggressive, although under no circumstances should this be misinterpreted as being nonfunctional as a lethal martial art.

Tai Chi's fundamental technique is *readiness.* To be ready means being alert and receptive. As a model, Lao-tzu notes in his fifteenth epistle,

> *The ancient masters were . . .*
> *Watchful like men crossing a winter stream.*
> *Alert, like men aware of danger . . .*
> *Yielding, like ice about to melt.*
>   —#15 (translated by Gia-Fu Feng and Jane English)

Tai Chi emphasizes basic readiness and a centered home-base position to work from. With correct footwork established, there are four critical techniques, or what might best be described as "postures," to master. Center of gravity is paramount in Tai Chi. The earth is our root and source of strength, so correct footwork is at the heart of acquiring mastery in the art. As an introduction, one should simply stand erect with the feet comfortably spaced a few inches apart. With arms held loosely at the side, one's armpit lines up vertically with, more or less, the outside of the foot. The head is held erect with the gaze trained comfortably ahead to a point on the ground approximately twelve feet away.

The first principle of correct Tai Chi posture is *Cham-kin*. This means "letting the shoulders drop." Standing erect, but without consciously forcing any part of the body into uncomfortable alignment, one lets the arms hang down straight with the palms of the hands resting against the upper thighs. There should be no sense of tension anywhere in the shoulder area. Avoidance of tensing up muscle areas is a key practice technique in Tai Chi, and is a devil to master.

Joy-jow, the second principle, means keeping the elbows tucked in toward the ribs and, whenever possible, pointed downward to the ground. This may seem as if basic arm movement is restricted, but it is not. Attentiveness to joy-jow prevents our elbows from losing their own rootedness to the ground, for once elbows flex horizontally they lose power and immediately engage tension in the shoulders. This in turn tightens up muscles in the neck and so on down the line. Even the smallest amount of tension is to be avoided, and joy-jow is a wonderfully practical reminder to stay focused.

Ham-hung, the third principle, concerns attentiveness to the "pelvic tilt." With shoulders relaxed, elbows tucked loosely to the sides, and forearms soft and limber, one now needs to contain the chi energy inhaled in breathing. This is done by lightly tucking in the tail of the spine and curving the rump inward. It will be significantly easier at this stage if your knees are also bent slightly. It will also seem reflexive at this point to begin tightening the stomach muscles but there is no need to do so: simply breathe. Air will naturally begin entering the abdominal area—what Tai Chi people call "the pocket." This is known as "letting your chi sink."

Ham-hung gives the lower body a slight curvature. To balance this, *Bat-bui,* the fourth principle, suggests shaping the upper back and shoulders ever so slightly to "convexity," or the general outline of a circle. As an approximation, one may raise a hand with the index finger near one's face. Straighten the fingers, then relax. They naturally take on a curvature. Shake the hand and let it find its natural comfort zone; that is more or less the ideal body working form from which to apply Tai Chi as self-defense.

Standing erect and following the four guides to posture hardly settles one into ideal combat positioning and, while there is much more, this is how one begins. As any capable instructor teaches, the legs must carry the load. Tai Chi, like most Asian martial arts, relies upon a flexed leg stance. Tai Chi movements stem from the *Ma* or "horse-seat" stance that can be described as follows.

From the basic feet-apart stance and beginning body posture detailed above, extend the space between the feet to shoulder width; this varies according to an individual's size, but about sixteen inches should suffice. Ensure that the knees are flexed. The hands now will hang nearer the inner thigh. This "sitting" posture is Ma.

Dividing the body's lower root-strength from its upper-torso softness in muscle and limb is the waist, an element of critical importance possessing its own extensive Tai Chi mythology. For now, however, one has achieved the basic Tai Chi "Earth-Centered Stance." A Western hybrid name I like for this rooted stance is "Standing Zazen," for one can train posture and leg strength while meditating from this position.

Once the knees and large thigh muscles become accustomed through regular exercise to the pressure of bearing body weight, it is possible to begin working toward real self-defense. Tai Chi works on yin-yang principles, and in practical terms this is understood as the concepts of "emptiness" and "fullness" in the shifting and deployment of body mass and weight.

It is the nature of water—the element Lao-tzu so often refers in describing Tao—not to resist:

> *Water gives life to the ten thousand things*
> *and does not strive.*
> *It flows in the places men reject and so is like the Tao. . . .*
> *Under heaven nothing is more soft and yielding than*
> *water.*
> *Yet for attacking the solid and strong, nothing is better.*
> *It has no equal.*
> —# 8 (translated by Gia-Fu Feng and Jane English)

Customarily, Tai Chi avoids direct attack. Whenever possible it deflects or channels an opponent's thrust away at an angle. This is what is meant by nonresistance. Should other methods of resolution come to naught, attack is avoided by shifting the mass and weight of the body away from the direction of the attack. In practical terms, this means one of two things: stepping backward, or away from the opponent's thrust, thereby physically removing oneself as an obstacle; or, deflecting the attack by turning the waist and shifting body mass in combination with some deflective action by the arms or feet. Tai Chi's basic readiness position against attack evolves directly from the Earth-Centered Stance. With one knee flexed, all the body weight is shifted onto that leg while the other "empty" foot rocks lightly forward and outward, resting on its heel approximately a foot ahead of the other load-bearing counterpart. While it is "empty" and bears no weight, the empty knee is also kept lightly flexed. Making slight adjustments to keep one's Ma seat comfortably aligned, one then "Raises up the Hands." This is a recognizable Tai Chi movement also known as *Play the Guitar,* or *Pipa.* With shoulders dropped and elbows in, one arm (let's say the right one) is rocked upward from the shoulder; bending the elbow, the hand is centered knife-edge outward (palm facing left) about fourteen inches in front of the face, with fingertips reaching no higher than the nose. The elbow, which has rocked forward from the body, points downward to the ground joy-jow style—not parallel.

For the left arm, raise the forearm upward from the thigh until the hand is held at the level of the corresponding right elbow now protecting the head. With a slight shift of the waist, the upper body rotates to the left four to six inches. With gaze fixed directly ahead on what might be coming, one has effectively "closed the gates" and is now prepared for the basic methods by which an opponent may attack: with hands (or weapon in hand), feet, or head. This then is Tai Chi readiness from which we can employ our blocks, arm bars, feints, pulls, hand and finger strikes, sweeps, thrusts, blows, trips, kicks, and sundry other techniques best left unmentioned.

12

THE FOUR PILLARS

I T WAS SUMMER AND I received a call from an out-of-town Tai Chi friend who was in Vancouver on business. We met and talked over coffee while he mentioned how he'd found yet another exciting new teacher in Seattle. Simon was investing much practice time of late, he said, and had made some break-throughs. Would I care to see a brief demonstration? Not wishing to appear inhospitable, I assented.

Performing a set, Simon's improvement was noticeable. His style was getting softer, moving up a notch or two. Still, I was surprised to see that every trace of four simple, connected move-ments called *Pa, Li, Jai, On* (block, twist, press, push) had been expunged from his practice.

"Why is that?" I asked.

"Too boring," he explained. "All that repetition, we don't bother with it."

Later, as I feared we must, we sparred together in a friendly way on the beach near my home. We've been at this for more than fifteen years and nothing much changes. We begin courteously, cautiously; then Simon's muscle kicks in and he presses. He is a strong man; his force can be alarming and requires great alertness to avoid being swept away. But using force entails risk as well, for if an opponent is not overpowered in the first attack—and if he or she understands counterattack—the aggressor himself is left at his most vulnerable. The key in sparring with such people is to attune as highly as possible to their energy and intentions, for if one survives their onslaught, then a quick counterstrike easily knocks them off balance—or worse, if necessary. Caesar details an identical strategy in *The Conquest of Gaul.* In almost every major battle his invading forces were badly outnumbered, yet as general he understood that if the ferocious first strikes of the Celts could be withstood or repulsed, the enemy lost heart and was quickly dispatched thereafter.

That morning we were barefoot and Simon brimmed with confidence. He struck hard, swiftly, but I managed to avoid his heavy thrust and the matter was soon concluded.

"How do you do it?" he asked, frustrated.

"It's the four movements you don't practice. A lot of other people ignore it as well. Sifu teaches that those four moves are the heart of our Tai Chi self-defense. That's why we practice them so often in the sets we play—they're in there to save yer bacon."

The Tai Chi boom in the West is not always kind. When instruction becomes linked to dollars and livelihoods there is a tendency among teachers to respond to complaints about boring repetition in Tai Chi by making deletions. Cutting corners is okay once in a while when the bus is leaving for work and we haven't quite finished our morning practice, but it provides a poor foundation for future growth. There is no mastery in shortcuts. Pa, Li, Jai, and On are four unspectacular movements. Beginning with the weight on the left leg, one then rocks forward onto the right, then shifts back left, and moves forward again on the right. There is little of the flowing beauty of *Grasp the Bird's Tail,* or *Golden Phoenix Greets the Sun* about them. With no flashy kicks, or the magic wandlike handwork of other moves, they are pedestrian in every way. They are also repeated at least seven times during three sets of the Yang long-form, which is most widely practiced in the West. Surely, there is a reason for that.

Pa is the blocking, or warding off, of an opponent's striking attack. The method is to step forward, shift the weight onto the rear leg, and sweep the right hand and arm up to intercept the opponent's strike. The attacking strike is met by our knife-edge forearm in the vicinity of the wrist bone. As the right arm sweeps upward, it is joined by the fingertips of the left hand, which raise to support the intercepting right. These left fingertips brace softly against the right wrist where it joins the right thumb and back up along the forearm.

Now, as one steps forward and makes contact with the attacking strike, at the same moment one turns the waist in the direction of the oncoming blow and sits lower with the weight-bearing leg. In this way, our interception of the blow becomes a deflection, warding it away from our vital center. Simultaneously, we rock forward onto our right leg, thrusting our weight upward from the ground through our left leg. Our left hand enters this thrust, so that as the opponent is moving through our right-hand side, we are now retaliating from the left. Our force drives upward from the ground and sweeps through our left forearm and shoulder. This inner power drives up from the muscles along the spine and is fueled by chi driven from our abdominal air pocket. The direction of our attack is by now the shoulder area of the opponent. Ideally, all of the aforementioned steps are accomplished with a smooth-flowing movement. Given the opponent's own speed and force, plus the shock of losing contact with the obstacle he or she has expected, our counterattack should succeed in cleaving the opponent off balance.

If, on being repulsed, he recovers from our counterforce and decides to attack once more, his likeliest action will be to plant his feet, then strike with his left fist.

We counter with Li, an arm bar. In this position we retreat

from the opponent's thrust. Our hands—which by now are in a position of left high, right low—reverse. As we roll back, the right hand raises itself to cheek height (imitating the wing sweep of the white crane/blue heron), and the left sinks a little. It is held diagonally, some ten inches before our breast. In effect, we have returned to the basic readiness position.

With the opponent's strike, we roll back onto our left leg. In this case, it is our left hand that makes contact with the opponent's strike. Again, we sit-leg and turn our waist as our left wrist guides away the attacking arm. The optimum contact point is in the area of the opponent's wrist and forearm. As we turn our waist in the direction of the blow—this time we are turning to the left—with the fingers of our left contact hand we gently rotate the opponent's arm; we are attempting to softly twist his elbow upward. Now, as we have been making contact and turning, the movement of our waist has automatically brought our right arm and hand into contact with the opponent's arm. The desired contact point is above the elbow. At this point, it is a matter of driving our chi through our right-arm force while gently supporting the opponent's arm with our left hand. For our opponent, the result is excruciating, causing either extreme hyperextension of the elbow joint, or a complete separation.

With skill, an opponent may yet dodge our Li defense and escape our arm bar. If he straightens up, or crowds us, we roll back and draw in our elbows while gathering our hands in loose fists at our breast. Left hand braces the right. This is Jai. Crouching, marshaling strength, we thrust upward forcefully in a mighty push. In this, we rock forward on our right knee. Our hands then unfold softly, left over right before us, centered about midpoint of our face. With our palms now facing us, and with arms softly outstretched, we expand and open our embrace shoulder-wide. If the opponent recklessly attacks again, we rock back on our left leg, allow him to enter our space, then simultaneously lower our center and swiftly draw in our arms. With elbows clinching to sides, we seize the opponent's limbs in a pincer movement, sit-leg yet further, then thrust upward and forward dramatically from our left leg. This is On. The effect is devastating. An opponent suddenly finds his limbs first seized, then jerked rapidly downward; this causes a natural snap of his head as he struggles to retain his vision. At that precise moment, he finds himself being driven backward with maximum force. On is the specific defense against push-in-the-chest bullying, or shirt-front grabbing, personal invasions. A variant also can be successfully applied one-handedly.

While Pa, Li, Jai, and On are practiced in series, their applications are endless. Blocking, retreating, warding off, and counterattacking constitute the very heart of Tai Chi's self-defense strategy. What must be grasped in mastering these difficult procedures is that several body movement processes are at work simultaneously. This is no small feat to accomplish and requires long study.

Advanced understanding of the four pillars is normally also complemented by knowledge of the *da lu,* or "four corners" established for maximum martial effectiveness. This consists of: *choi,* a movement in which we grasp the opponent by the hand and, with a turn of waist and stance, haul him down and away from our center; *lay,* a spinning open-hand type chop or cut that is effected by reversing the movement of choi; *jow,* a timely strike using the elbow utilized in close-in encounters such as push-hands, which is effective against sudden attacks on our person; and *kow,* another "close-to-the-belt" fighting technique in which we deliver a thump using our shoulder. These are extremely useful techniques that may be employed convincingly against such threats as urban muggings.

To these must be added an understanding of several theoretical principles that, while seemingly abstract, are, in fact, elemental to Tai Chi self-defense strategy. *Jim, nim,* and *lim* detail the process of making contact with an opponent and cleaving to his spirit.

Jim is adherence, making contact with arm or wrist to the opponent's arm or wrist for the purposes of detecting the flow, power, and direction of his energy. Any movement on our part occurs as intuitive response to such information.

Nim means sticking, never breaking contact with the opponent. By cleaving to his spirit we avoid the chaos of unpredictability.

Lim is an extension of nim and means "to follow"; should the opponent attempt feints or even withdraw, we maintain constant contact, never allowing him to escape our stickiness. These three jewels—jim, nim, and lim—were adopted as the guiding principles of Vietnamese guerrilla combat strategy during the Indochinese War.

Not everyone shares a taste for such martial applications and this is understandable. All of the above techniques require personal instruction and dedicated study. For many practitioners, perhaps even the majority, what is important in their Tai Chi is health, exercise, and meditation. Through the years though, especially in teaching situations, older citizens—women especially— have inquired about certain, quick-study self-defense techniques, and it is a fact that there are several available from within the Tai Chi arsenal. Good instructors deduce the right intentions in these situations fairly quickly and should be capable of providing the necessary information.

13

FIVE ELEMENTS: THE WEB OF INTERCONNECTION

P A, LI, JAI, AND On enjoy alchemical correspondences in Taoist cosmology that are noteworthy for their physiological and medical affinities. The first four "development phases" of the Ba Gwa's universal energy, Pa, Li, Jai, and On, are complemented by the four previously discussed martial applications of choi, lay, jow, kow. Combining to form the eight steps of Taoism's powerful Tai Chi circle, these development phases are a further means by which primal chi energy is made manifest.

When we play Tai Chi, we give expression through our physical movements to the eight developmental phases of energy transmission. By their very nature, the eight steps are external, self-directed expressions of our own internal chi energy. This inner energy is received in turn through the cultivation of our physical and insight, or meditation, training. In effect, we become transmitters through which external chi is channeled inward and redirected again to the larger universe. When we are healthy and in attunement with the prevailing natural forces, the chi flows smoothly throughout our body and is returned to the void through our breath or other physical expressions. Understanding how this process functions enables advanced practitioners of Tai Chi to begin channeling their positive internal chi in two ways: inwardly, through their own body and organs; and externally, projecting it for the purposes of Chi Kung healing in others, or for self-defense.

A further series of steps also assists direction of our inner energy with rather obvious physical manifestations. From midpoint in a circle, they represent movement either stepping forward, backward, left, or right, or "keeping still" in holding to the centerpoint. For notation purposes, North, South, East, West, and the Center or Earth still-point are commonly used.

Each of these directional expressions of energy transmission is highly symbolic and associated with one of the five traditional Chinese alchemical formulations of primal matter: earth, air, fire, water, and metal. In correct proportion—in balance—these five elements comprise matter that is in harmony with the greater world beyond. Out of balance, an excess or insufficiency creates disharmony or, in a medical sense, disease.

Taoist cosmology attributes a totality of bodily functions, tastes, emotions, probable illnesses, strengths, and colors, as well as animal and spiritual characteristics to the five elements.

Rightly, it is a study in itself and is affiliated with a branch of Taoist practice concerned with divination via the *I Ching*, or Book of Changes, known as *feng shui* (the study of spatial/ supernatural relationships between objects), as well as with Chinese medicine.

In the Taoist mind the universal flow of chi is ceaseless and cyclical. It enters our body through the breathing process and circulates down through the inner organs, through the abdomen, through the limbs, through the perineum region, and back up the spine to the crown of the head. As we breathe and progress through our Tai Chi movements, it is useful in terms of aligning our posture to imagine a golden thread connecting this crown point with heaven.

In playing Tai Chi it helps to be mindful of the correspondences existing between our physical movements and the effect they exert upon the circulation of our chi through the major inner organs and lymphatic system. The five directional energies are identified in Taoist thought with certain fundamental characteristics that are represented as follows:

Direction:	Element:	Major Organ:
South	Fire	Heart/blood/small intestine
North	Water	Kidney/bladder/genitals
East	Wood	Liver/gall bladder

West	Metal	Lungs/nervous system/large intestine
Center	Earth	Stomach/pancreas/spleen

It is efficacious when playing Tai Chi to be mindful of the stimulative effects rendered by our movement in specific sequences upon various organs. From a health perspective, it is also helpful to consider the seasonal values attributed to the directional energies:

Direction:	*Season:*
South	Summer
North	Winter
East	Spring
West	Autumn
Center	"Indian summer"/transition from summer to autumn

In this way for example, during the late autumn and winter periods when colds, respiratory problems, and aching backs and bones are most common, one is able to consciously and benevolently channel real healing energy toward the chest and lower back areas while playing Tai Chi. For its part, feng shui is often called "the art of placement" and while exercising, as our circulation deepens, it is beneficial to mentally project energy toward an uncomfortably knotted shoulder or rotating joint.

The longer we stay with our Tai Chi practice, the more our consciousness of Taoism's web of interconnection expands. From nature's visible progress of the seasons and the nighttime cycle of the heavenly constellations, to growing awareness of birdlife, the community of smaller critters around us at all times, and increased sensitivity to our own inner physical balance—all this and more comes to enrich both our silent practice and the unfolding of our days on Mother Earth. With wu-wei, noneffort, continual patterns of order reveal themselves organically and unbidden amid the everyday ups and downs of this ephemeral world. We need use only our five senses to be mindful as we flow through our five animal-inspired series of movements, our Tai Chi, in overcoming the modern distractions that each new morning brings.

14

WHAT WE DON'T THINK ABOUT IN TAI CHI

I T IS NATURAL TO encounter distractions of mind while playing Tai Chi. Distraction arises in everyone's meditation. Immediately prior to his enlightenment, the Buddha Shakyamuni was tempted by Mara the Evil One near the Naranja River. Meditating in Gethsemane, Jesus of Nazareth implored, "Father, take this cup of suffering from me." There are no exceptions.

The ideal Tai Chi state is "No-Mindedness," or Emptiness, but since random, discontinuous thoughts throw themselves up on the mind-screen spontaneously while we practice, dealing with them effectively is a matter of technique. Most Asian forms of meditation rely on breath as a means of dispatching spontaneous mind-chatter. Both the Northeast Asian Mahayana and South and Southeast Asian Hinayana Buddhist schools instruct students to concentrate on the in-breath as a way to clear distracting thoughts. Meditation is a discipline and by focusing on the physical act of inhaling breath right down into our abdomen, stray thoughts are quickly dispelled.

Tibetan Vajrayana Buddhism provides us with a different, more energetic approach: concentration on the *out*-breath. In this way, distractions in mind are released in concert with the lungs. Either method is suitable.

As a moving meditation, Tai Chi offers a third approach. When distracting thoughts arise during our routine, we acknowledge them in a kindly way and return to focus on our moving hand. Simply train the mind's eye on the palm of the hand wherever it may be. The result is instantaneous. Distraction falls away of itself.

It has been a sentimental gesture among poets, scholars, and dharma hands at least since the time of Plato to sigh at the world's reflection of "these fallen times." Walkman radios, cathode-ray tubes, cell phones, the lot: technology is relentless in its assault upon simple quietude. Often it may seem as if there are people walking around who have forgotten what silence is, who no longer know what it is, or are afraid of it. Theoretically, it could be possible that one day God, or the Tao, or Gaia, or just plain old Shunyata emptiness will be revealed through a new and improved multimedia manufactured Samsara device, but I wouldn't hold my breath waiting for it to happen. It's simpler to just breathe.

So, grasshopper, what are you looking for?

When trying to name the unnameable, it's helpful to recognize what we're *not* looking for. One of my favorite "Zen Is Not Zen" parables comes from Paul Reps and Nyogen Senzaki's indispensable little book *Zen Flesh, Zen Bones.* In a nutty tale entitled "Learning to Be Silent" they report the following:

> *The pupils of the Tendai school used to study meditation before Zen entered Japan. Four of them who were intimate friends promised one another to observe seven days of silence.*
>
> *On the first day all were silent. Their meditation had begun auspiciously, but when night came and the oil lamps were growing dim one of the pupils could not help exclaiming to a servant: "Fix those lamps."*
>
> *The second pupil was surprised to hear the first one talk. "We are not supposed to say a word," he remarked.*
>
> *"You two are stupid. Why did you talk?" asked the third.*
>
> *"I am the only one who has not talked," concluded the fourth pupil.*

If only he'd taken another deep breath, or focused intently on his hand!

15

HANGING LOOSE WITH SIFU

ONCE IN A WHILE, Sifu and I duck out on the world, have lunch, and hang loose together. It's special to eat with an old man like him because there's so much to learn: the fastidious way he studies a menu; his careful etiquette of eating and digesting; even the last mindful look-see a teacher like Sifu conducts among restaurant tables and chairs to ensure nothing is left behind. Everything done to completion.

Vancouver is a harbor city, and jutting out from its central core into English Bay is the huge forest reserve of Stanley Park. A seawall promenade encircles the park for seven kilometers or so, and the city's fabled natural beauty—sea, mountains, and forests—is all on display. It's a great place for strolling with a friend.

It was October, and we drove downtown one afternoon and parked the car beside the water. Sifu checked everything over twice, and we set off. Our route led up a broad footpath by the bay, and we headed toward Second Beach farther along the park. As we ambled, we swapped news—any old thing, really:

chance remarks, bits of this and that in our shared, pidgin dialect. Sifu pointed at the jeweled glint of autumn sun on the water, sizing up its photographic possibilities. I kept an eye out for the herons that fished among huge rocks on the shoreline. Unaccountably, passersby seldom notice these awesome creatures until they are pointed out to them.

On the bay, freighters tugged at anchor beneath the northern mountains, and early winter bands of wood ducks, surf scoters, and gulls hovered among the tidal shoals offshore. Continuing along, we marched together and saw wild ivy turning vermilion on the rocky ledges above the pathway.

Sifu talked about Tai Chi. "Conceal it," he said, hands deep in his overcoat pockets. "Don't let other people know what you know."

That's Tai Chi, I had heard. Ordinary, anonymous, like a man in plain clothes in a crowd. Taoist masters are emphatic about secrecy: no shouting about things—no black belts, yellow belts; no exhibitions, no competitions. They teach us their techniques and tools, then one day leave us in the marketplace to fend for ourselves. Just mind your business, they say. If you need your training, let it strike like a thunderclap—unexpectedly, like the jaws of a dragon.

At Second Beach, the sands broaden out. Where the seawalk

begins to narrow a little and less adventuresome visitors decide they've had enough, a fish-and-chip's shop and a playground for the kids appear. There are benches for resting, and one overhears the babble of a dozen different tongues. Sifu and I paused here as the world passed by: Rollerbladers in leotards, without helmets; joggers in hot-pink, sporting Walkmans; rambling lovers; the elderly, and the lonely.

Sifu nodded as a powerful Rollerblader clipped past: *"Mo Yang,"* he said. "No good. He use too much muscle. Must only use soft." Cocking his head slightly to one side, he pointed left-handed with his index and middle fingers in sword style for emphasis. His fine, soft skin still riffled when he laughed. With so many active models scooting past us, Sifu discoursed for fun on kinetics. He was, of course, talking Tai Chi. Setting off again, I studied him as he admired the overhanging roots and stumps along the rocky slopes above the trail. A tiny, vibrant dragon with almond eyes and high cheekbones.

At Third Beach, twenty minutes farther on, we bought cups of coffee and stood along together on a rise overlooking the sea: an old man and his disciple talking shop above the sandbars. Sifu pointed to the sandstone massifs beyond, at the Day-Glo algae on shady rocks, and the watery rivulets coursing through clefts, vines, and leaves. As the sun sank lower, so we shifted from the chill into brighter patches where light still pursed through the bowl of trees, talking with our hands, listening to each other patiently.

Sifu talked about the olden days: about China, his Shanghai family, and of traveling to the emperor's gardens at Hangzhou. He recounted the story of his flight from Mao Zedong; and how on hearing his relations had been killed by the Reds, he'd swum by night, middle-aged, into British Hong Kong to survive selling noodles and jewelry. Now here he was in another world: Canada, North America.

Sifu said that he'd been born in 1904 when China was under the Manchu dynasty. The eldest of three children in a family of shopkeepers, he'd begun his schooling at age six. Education, then, consisted of the Chinese classics—Confucius, Mencius, books of Odes and Histories. Ethics was the root of a Chinese education.

As a youth, he had moved to Shanghai, he said, and this was where he began his Tai Chi training. It was more affordable than other pursuits requiring costly equipment. Apprenticed to a jeweler, he studied the craft for five years and this enabled him to marry and take a wife. Already though, civil war had begun. The Kuomintang government founded by Dr. Sun Yat-Sen in 1911 battled warlords, then the growing threat of Mao's Communists.

Sifu was in a talkative mood this day, and I had my notepad

handy—for years I'd been obliged to write down terms and words from the Chinese for later research and translation. There was one subject I'd wanted to bring up for a long time. I asked him about his lineage.

"What?" he questioned.

"Where you come from. Who were your teachers?"

To my good fortune, this sparked him in the right direction. I was anxious myself to know by what genealogy I'd arrived at this teaching of his from far-off China. Sifu began a labored explanation and I struggled to get down the list of names that transpired.

While in Shanghai, and later in Nanking, Sifu expounded, he found his great root teacher, Loy Ching-Yuen, with whom he studied meditation and healing in the Southern Mountain tradition for more than fifteen years. His Tai Chi instructor, however, was the accomplished Master Tin Siu-lin, who has since been written about in a number of books. Master Tin, as he is widely known, was one of several students of the legendary Master Yang Shao-hou (1861–1930), eldest son of Master Yang Chien-hou (1841–1917). The latter man, Sifu continued, was third son of Master Yang Lu-chan, known as Yang the Unsurpassable (1798–1872), of Hubei province, from whom as many books and pamphlets acknowledge the modern Yang style of Tai Chi Chuan descends. Yang Lu-chan himself was initiated by Master Chen Chang-hsing, known as Master Ancestor Tablet, of Hunan province. Here, after six generations, the traceable lineage ends, although two further teachers, dates uncertain, have survived in memory and are acknowledged by Master Ng: Wong Jung-Ngok and Jung Fat. Several Tai Chi "Classics" also exist and are available in a number of translations. Other than this, Tai Chi Chuan descends as a formal path from the legendary Taoist monk Chang San-feng, who composed his *Tai Chi Chuan Lun*, or "The Tai Chi Analects," during the Sung dynasty, circa A.D. 1200.

To hear this and write it all down was like meeting my own distant relatives. The Yang family saga has been often repeated, and Tin Siu-lin was a name I'd encountered more than once in my research. I had a lineage now. I knew who I was, from farther back at least than my parents' own families.

I had never walked with Sifu as far as Siwash Rock, a jagged stone Priapus that juts dramatically from the sea near the gateway channel to Vancouver's inner harbor. Today was clearly the right day. The wind whipped cold through the narrow neck of water, and already a thin layer of ice filmed the rock face. Meltwater glistened in the fading light, transforming the rock into a fantastic creation, alive and glowing. Lichens and algae glowed on every loose shard and crevice.

Sifu noticed a pair of small, worn metal plaques. One paid homage to a young diver who'd lost his life there in an accident. The second explained the aboriginal legend of how the rock got its name. I reported the story for my old teacher, of how Skalish, known as the Unselfish One, was transformed by Q'uas the Creator into this imperishable monument as a symbol of selflessness and regard for others. From ancient times onward, it has always been a holy place.

Sifu, as I'd reckoned, was impressed by this legend. It was almost Confucian, universal in emotion. We'd swapped histories.

We were hours together, Sifu and I, that late autumn afternoon. Two mornings later, we were back at our practice. No more yakking. Only teacher and students, moving in rhythm like shadows after the ox. Like water flowing over the mill.

16

WHERE THREE DREAMS CROSS

I T WAS SUMMER, EARLY July, and my wife and I dawdled through the morning, watching overcast skies for any break in the weather. Hitting the beach seemed an unlikely option.

Stir-crazy with inactivity, by one o'clock we made a move. Since a day at the beach was off, we'd try the mountains. An hour and a half later, with only light packs, we were well on the way to Cypress Bowl, with its jagged trail to Black Mountain Peak.

With each quarter hour, the weather grew more mawkish; overripe clouds threatened rain or even thunder. But occasionally in spots, the muggy haze was pierced by sunlight, and the prospect of the snowcapped ridges ahead made a few mountain hours too tempting to resist. Following a switchback, we glanced out upon the vast metropolis spread below, a vista ranging clear to the American border at Semiahmoo Bay more than twenty miles off.

Farther along, the guttural booms of a big male grouse thumped lonely on the cool, somber air. Then at three thousand feet, we watched, amazed, as a red-tailed hawk powered through the sky above the alpine valley beyond us, swooping the thermals, working the ridge for prey.

An hour later, we hit summer snowline. A meltwater brook surged from out of dense brush and we tramped after it to drink at the clean, crystal source. Heading back to the trail, my Asian wife said she'd feared that a tiger might have jumped us by surprise. All the Orient's best childhood myths involve tigers.

"No need worrying about either of those," I smiled. "There's nothing but mountain lions around this time of year."

Marching higher in the territory of a second booming grouse, we paused to eat a handful of trail mix. A trekker's hut perched on log stilts nearby. Again the grouse boomed, and tracing his calls we saw him roosting in the crick of a jack pine until he flew off to darker cover.

We set off again. From there on, the way was sodden and we traveled with caution. A shifty patch of trail had been shored up with rough planking, the thaw-holes beneath betraying meltwater rivulets. A wrong step meant a tumble into near-frozen, boggy mush. In poor light, we trucked farther through dense alpine forest, and the wilderness path grew difficult to discern. Trusting the colored trail tags marked high on guide trees, we pushed patiently onward.

After a last cover of pines, we arrived at the summit. No signage, no announcement; we were simply there. Beyond us lay huge horizons. We stood above everything. Occasionally, a small aircraft flew well below us, as turbulent vapors clouded the sun.

Enjoying the rare moment, we sat side by side on the bare granite knoll. Small pine and scrub flecked the summit, and about the edges lay a carpet of moss. Leaving packs aside, we stretched on our backs and gazed up at the show of clouds.

Soon, blackflies were biting. I rose and bundled twigs for a fire, which sparked to life on a bare spot of rock. I added damp leaves to make smoke. Opening a flask of tea, we munched on hard-boiled eggs and sweet nectarines. All around us, the stillness was profound. Eyes half-closed, we lay back again, so much nearer heaven.

We must have dozed, for soon the light declared it was time to descend. Setting off, we hacked down to the west as a low, golden light reflected off the ridges. We saw it then while stumbling onto an unkempt clearing. Simultaneously, we were struck speechless. Catching our breath, we moved nearer the apocryphal vision.

Before us lay a spectacular bowl, the natural convergence of three snow-clad peaks. The setting sun was now trained on this remote, open space, while boiling upward through the ethers an ocean of vapors surged forth, rising formlessly, opalescent, pulsing with life. Furling and unfurling, cloud-hidden to the world, the immutable Void of a hundred ancient parables danced before us, a kind of volcanic updraft of primordial chi, ceaselessly merging and reemerging in fantastic whorls of energy. Agape, we looked upon its transcendent power as it steamed from the vast depths below. There could be no higher purity, no greater *paramita* than this, expressing unfathomable nature here in the higher heights, sanctifying and elucidating mystically, silently, namelessly, its holy and perfect beyondness. The prayer came forth unbidden:

> *O precious vessel, unknowable source of the ten thousand*
> *things!*
> *Great Tao,*
> *The Jewel in the Lotus!*
> *Om Mane Padme Hum!*

17

THE PARADISE VARIATIONS

I'D BEEN TRAINING WITH Sifu for three years when my wife and I were led to Hawaii on a low-key commercial assignment. Arriving at Maui, we expected a tropical paradise. To our horror, our new island digs resembled nothing so much as a suburban condo project with tropical landscapes added for color and effect. Our next step was obvious.

On a tip, we made a hurried departure, setting off next morning with our bags and a sack of cold beer. Hitching through the cane fields, by day's end our good luck held and we came upon an isolated hamlet that was every inch a blessed and healing place where we were made welcome.

To our minds, we'd found paradise. So settled, we rented a shack by the bay replete with lush jungle and orchids at the door. Each day, I rose quietly and went fishing for our dinner. Heralded by an unimaginable chatter of birds, dawn comes early in the backcountry with the sun rising east from the sea. The humid morning air is alive with the chatter of songbirds, from which emerge wilder, guttural *wahoooos!*, shattering the primeval heaviness.

One morning, as usual, I made my way up the lane to an unused jetty. The hour was calm, the sugar mill abandoned. Across the bay, coco palms swayed in the breeze. Patiently, I cast out my line, trying baits without much success. Content for the while to let the line dangle, I surveyed my surroundings. The breeze was young and the waves tolled in nicely without any great force. Not a soul stirred ashore. It was magic and I thought of Django Reinhardt—his "Mystery Pacific." Is this what he'd meant, after all?

It was a perfect, tropical occasion to move the chi and I paced off my space on the old wartime dock. Breathing steadily, deeply, I commenced moving. Growing sure of my footing, I progressed through the movements, sweeping to the right and *Grasping the Bird's Tail.* Rocking softly in reverse, and stepping lightly to the left, I caught a glimpse of the land and sea. Shallow whispers blew in from the bay, then something unfamiliar began. From the open ocean I sensed my old master rise before me like a presence.

Breathing, I felt his spirit enter and move through my limbs. I let his presence flow of itself, and as I moved, my posture and expression attuned themselves with a softness and fullness I had never previously known. The chi was moving, I knew; more palpably than anything I'd experienced before—a steady magnetic pulse through my limbs and torso. I understood in that moment it was Sifu who directed its course. I moved about the jetty and he showed me the way: the ripple of his fingers unfolding in space; the weightless sinking of his sweeps and feints; the inward turning of a heel; or the effortless thrust of a knife-edge hand.

What I had seen with my eyes for the past three years was transpiring within my own being with only this sense of occurrence. No thinking; none at all, for the merest intimation might dissolve the visit spontaneously. Only movement, being present, full attentiveness. Breathing as the body wished.

"Don't think," Sifu taught. "Only move." No-mindedness as the way to mindfulness, I heard him saying.

The changes progressed: *Raise Hands Up, Slap the Face, White Stork Spreads Its Wings.* I sensed the old man very clearly, his visage blank of expression, moving like a frond in the wind. No resistance.

The litany of Yang forms and mudras worked on, transforming and completing itself as a course. Late in the second set I became aware that I was flying solo again, although Sifu had been there; that I knew. I played through to completion, rooted in fullness and harmony with the Tao. As I concluded—*Carry Tiger Back to Mountain*—there was emptiness: Perfect Tao. Immanent. Holy. All One.

My life altered in Hawaii, there by the sea, but I did not dwell on it. The heron dance I knew, itself had changed, transformed by a wholeness beyond physical form or self. Clearly, something had coursed through my limbs and like those struck by lightning, an indefinable cognizance has remained ever since. As Lao-tzu says:

Though I do not know its name, for lack of a better word,
I call it Tao.

—# 25 (translated by Gia-Fu Feng and Jane English)

18

TOY-SHOU: PUSH-HANDS

"Tom," Sifu said. "He wants to fight. But he can't fight. He uses muscle."

THE USE OF FORCE is avoided at all times when playing Tai Chi. Softness and relaxation, the physical equivalents of Lao-tzu's watercourse path of yieldingness, are paramount in Tai Chi practice.

"Softness" implies the absence of force in our movements and can be maddeningly difficult to achieve. It is a matter of degrees. Just when we feel we are finally floating free without the least use of muscle, our teacher may point us out with a small touch, and there, unmistakably we note the resistance. Truly, there is no genuinely perfect expression of Tai Chi, save perhaps the cry of birth and the sigh of a peaceful death. Serious followers of the path come to recognize certain moments, however, when the universe smiles and we find ourselves weaving at the margins of perfection. Why else put up with the bother of it all?

Tai Chi practice can also be wonderfully self-deceptive. While we practice, softness is always at the forefront of our mind, although within our performance, and even within our own attentiveness, it is likely that the use of muscle creeps in unawares. Partly due to simple fatigue, muscles can tighten up through overexertion, which is another way of saying that we've been using muscle all along, however gently. More than likely, it is a matter of our technique and level of accomplishment.

Tai Chi evolved as a form of moving yoga and meditation. Rooted in a core syllabus of unshakeable physical and metaphysical principles, it is still a developing art. The physical execution of its animal-inspired postures is an exacting science unmatched by few things known to the West. Ballet, competitive floor gymnastics, high alpine rock-climbing, the footwork of boxer Muhammad Ali in his prime, and perhaps Olympic-caliber figure skating are the nearest approximations that come to mind. Those who shaped Tai Chi Chuan worked to create a sacred dance form in which, as *The Diamond Sutra* declares, no ego, personality, or being continues to exist as a separated individuality from the unity of absolute reality. As students of the Tai Chi path, it is our task, like *The Diamond Sutra* declares of the bodhisattva, to develop "a pure, lucid mind, not depending upon sound, flavor, touch, odor, or any quality . . . a mind that alights upon nothing whatsoever."

There is only one way this can be accomplished: through sheer nonresistance. Only through wu-wei can the chi flow unhindered through our body and return to its elemental source. The ultimate aim of Tai Chi is to dispense with muscular stiffness or resistance of any sort that might impede the flow of chi during our exercise. The way that advancing students learn to detect muscle resistance in themselves and others is by playing *Toy-shou,* "Push-hands."

Push-hands practice cultivates the active-reactive awareness upon which the spiritual and martial vision of Tai Chi is founded. Once we develop our basic stance and posture, the use of muscle is likeliest to manifest in our arms. The exercise is devised for two partners, although once we understand the techniques involved, we can also play toy-shou alone, but this is a less interesting alternative.

Push-hands assumes that the partners in the exercise are intent on training their personal balance by connecting with their partner at the wrist(s) and alternately rocking forward and backward from the knees. While turning the waist and rotating the torso in a circular motion as we rock forward—*kung-toy*—and back—*jaw-toy*—we deliver pressure of various strengths against the opponent. This pressure, or force, is not muscular in nature. Rather, it follows the principles of the lever: force, mass, lift, thrust, trajectory, and so forth—the essential laws of aerodynamics. Like gravity, all this can be delivered without the overt use of muscular power. With a good stance, we are able to withstand the "attacking" force of our partner, while our countering force arises both from the earth and from the opponent's own skewed attack, which our technique will turn against him.

Superficially, the "object" of our repetitive manipulations is to knock our opponent off balance; the real skill lies in not being knocked off balance ourselves when we are "attacked." From our rooted ma stance, our chi is expressed through the arms and hands, and when desirable, by our elbows (jow), shoulders (kow), hips, etc. Tai Chi is the harmony of yin and yang energies. As we push forward against our opponent, we express yang energy. Withdrawing, we express yin. As Sifu Ng explains, the lower half of the body is our strong foundation. Rooted firmly to the ground through our stance, we can remain supple and reflexive in the upper body—yin resting on yang. Above the waist, our torso, head, and limbs are like a floating blossom that moves harmoniously with the pivoting action of our waist and the rise and fall of our flexed-knee stance.

By nature, all Tai Chi movements are executed without conscious thought. There is a reason for the repetitive practice of various techniques associated with every martial art, whether Eastern, Western, African, South Indian, or the like. Repetition numbs the mind while simultaneously honing the execution of particular actions. Through daily training, performance that is unfettered by intellection—by thought—becomes automatic. Should negative situations arise without warning, we are trained to react spontaneously in a skillful mode. In Tai Chi training, we endeavor to attain balance and grace. It is a working with stillness, for only through stillness can we cultivate active/reactive awareness. There is no other way. What is this special awareness? It is a strategy, an almost unconscious adaptability to negative situations as they arise. Should this take the form of an attack against our person, simultaneous with our realization of what is transpiring against us, our response is already in progress. Nothing prepares us for this eventuality like push-hands, and for this reason it is practiced at great length by Tai Chi people.

As Musashi the peerless Japanese swordsman details in his remarkable *Book of Five Rings,* the true exponent of the martial arts must comprehend fully and must master an opponent's spirit. All possible combinations inherent in the opponent's mind, whether offensive, defensive, or reactive, must be anticipated and understood. The successful martial exponent becomes a shadow warrior: the opponent thrusts, we withdraw; he pushes hard, using muscle—we rock back, sit-leg, turn the waist, adjust our footing, and, synchronizing energy through all these steps, we counter the attack. As the enemy moves, so we define our response: when the force of attack is delivered against us, we are not there. This is the knowledge of "Critical Moment Self-Defense."

19

CRITICAL-MOMENT SELF-DEFENSE

MASTER NG SAYS, "IF A MAN COMES, I GO AWAY. IF HE MOVES AWAY, I PUSH AGAINST HIM."

THERE IS ANOTHER GREAT secret that one learns pushing hands. It is called "Seizing the Critical Moment." Now, between offense and defense, offense is learned most easily in the martial arts. The basic mechanics of "attack" can be learned from observing any dog fight: sudden aggression, distracting barks or movement, overwhelming force. This is the way of nature.

Defense is another matter. It is a product of thought, study, and analysis: an acquired skill. Successful defense is holistic— true skill relies upon reading both the human and physical landscapes that inspire our reaction. Critical-moment defense is another matter entirely. It is a raw survival technique acquired through long training and is utilized intuitively against surprise attack, or as our last resort if first-line defense fails.

In desperate situations, there is no spare nanosecond for thought. Critical-moment defense kicks in at the micropoint in time when we realize we are poised on the razor edge of oblivion.

If we are physically set upon, the natural animal reaction is emotional—fear, terror, the urge to flee, anger, vengeance, what have you. Veteran Tai Chi people speak though of maintaining a "cool heart" even in the direst circumstances.

"Cool-Heart Tai Chi" is the supreme moment in combat, whether ritualized in school training or in the everyday jumble of the streets. It symbolizes the softness and relaxation that must take precedence at the still point of our gravest personal danger. To react otherwise in dire moments is to stiffen against attack, to use muscle—in other words, to actively resist the aggressor. Such defense may succeed if backed by brute force; yet, were we to have it at our disposal, it is unlikely an attack would occur in the first place. Lacking such force, the result of late physical resistance is almost inescapable: disarray, defeat, and chaos.

Within the divination system associated with the *I Ching* oracle, however, is a concept known as the turning point. This is understood as a critical transformational point in the flow and flux of cosmic energies that influence certain worldly events. At any given point, subtle shiftings of these cosmic energies may exert change in the cycles and tides of fortune. By attuning our personal actions synchronistically with the larger cosmic order, it becomes possible for us as individuals to exert a role in the transformation of chaos into opportunity. In a martial sense, this translates as shifting our fate from catastrophe to salvation.

This is how it is effected. On being attacked skillfully or suddenly, at the point we are in maximum danger of being physically overcome, we intuitively reverse away from the enemy's attack with a sharp turn of our waist, shift of our wrist, or lightning-fast bob of our knee(s), which immediately lowers or shifts our center of gravity. In the ideal conception, these moves are accomplished simultaneously. At the critical moment when the adversary's aggressive thrust howls past, or over us, we anneal our own bone-snapping energy to its force and send the aggressor careening where he will.

"Easy to say; hard to do," Master Ng explains.

In truth, I never fully understood this teaching until I saw it for myself one evening in Chinatown. Still early in my apprenticeship, I faithfully journeyed the twelve miles each Tuesday and Friday evening to Chinatown, where for two hours or more, whatever the season, we worked out, training and exercising incessantly under Sifu's implacably corrective eye. At ten o'clock as the women in the group took their leave, the street doors were locked and the remaining six or seven men got down to sparring, pushing hands, and getting salty, fathoming out attacks and counters, feints, and studying the manifold hard styles of the Orient and how to deal with them as opponents.

I'd been the sole *lo-fan* Westerner of either gender for a long time until we were joined by Errol, a thickset West Indian, and it grew my lot to spar with him ad infinitum, defending long hours against his heavy physical force.

Among Sifu's group was a Cantonese engineer named Tom with a passion for exploring other martial schools and teachers for exotic new methods and ideas. He had a muscular approach and, while affable, never managed to break through to the higher levels of accomplishment he sought. In quieter moments, Sifu said Tom jumped around too much; no matter how good the teacher, he never stayed anywhere long enough to scratch past the surface of any tradition. Perhaps there was something to it. Over time, even low men on the totem pole like Errol and I began besting Tom in push-hand sessions. Tom began appearing less frequently. When he did attend, though, he talked up a new style he'd discovered—"Water-boxing."

Late one Friday evening as the doors were being locked, Tom arrived with a friend.

It was unusual to admit a stranger at such a late hour when serious fighting techniques were under the microscope, but Tom began chatting informally, smoothing out a welcome. In his usual fashion, he made the rounds, pushing hands here and there with various students. Between sessions, he attempted conversation with Sifu, but not much was happening any longer between them. Then Tom sparred with big Errol and received a lesson. Errol's arm bars jammed the lighter man repeatedly and left Tom red in the face and flustered.

"He's never really bought into Sifu's softness," Errol mumbled in an aside as Tom struggled through another round or two. Then the newcomer peeled off his jacket and walked over. My Chinese protocol was pretty thin. No one seemed to recognize him, but his coiled strength and well-honed trim were readily visible. Tom introduced him as a water-boxer.

"He is very adept," Tom added.

What followed was extraordinary and nothing at all like *The Karate Kid*. The newcomer engaged Chung, our number two–ranked student, and overpowered him with embarrassing ease. His handwork in particular was extremely sophisticated, like a flensing knife.

He moved with an animal grace, toying with one or two other Chinese students until Tom introduced him to Mah, Sifu's top student, and a young master himself. Mah the invincible. This would be a real test.

Mah never had a chance. Every move and turn he made was parried, jammed, then rammed home against him. The interloper's long arms and taut-as-a-bow-string physique drew Mah in like an insect. The stranger's dominance was absolutely comprehensive; Mah could never establish his own position. As their sparring went on, the water-boxer flexed his strength and Mah understood himself to be in real danger. With quiet dignity, he disengaged with a nod of concession.

A certain menace descended upon the training hall. Accordingly, the stranger glowered in appropriate fashion, not strutting, but supremely cocky. Errol and I looked on with some trepidation. "He's some gunslinger," Errol said. It was disturbing and I wondered how these things finished themselves in Chinatown, in the upstairs back rooms of another world. An ugly vibration had entered the room and one sensed there'd be no walking out the door unchallenged. It was all unpleasantly familiar from the worst old days of high-school thuggery and muggery. We were in a bad, bad real-life movie.

The stranger's silence and control of the situation were unsettling. I mulled over what they might be about; it felt like we were in for a shakedown, some sort of takeover. To think of losing Sifu's family-like arrangements here was intolerable.

I locked dead-eye with the newcomer, raising my hands in challenge with thoughts of how a sudden street-kicking strike might end the ugliness. He raised his hands. Sifu's wrist cut through smartly. "No, Mr. Trevor," he said quietly, squaring himself off against the stranger.

"Toy-shou," he said calmly. Push-hands.

The newcomer stepped forward, making contact with Sifu.

Wrists and forearms worked single-handed in wide, fluid circles, rocking and withdrawing rhythmically as they gauged each other's form and reach. From the first, the newcomer's strength and flexibility presented a great challenge to our teacher. Stilled by the tension, the entire room watched on. The minutes passed as the two of them established their ground; the stranger, younger and stronger, controlling the critical middle space, cramping Sifu into tight areas against his increasingly powerful thrusts.

The only sound was the steady whir of air and chafing of their clothing as they brushed against each other. The contest went on a long time and as the wall clock ticked away, the interloper gathered strength, redoubling his attacks. The old master seemed harried. Glances of concern passed through the group as it actually appeared possible that our teacher might be defeated. It was an alarming notion. What would happen then?

The tempo of the contest grew; the stranger took over. Sifu was simply hanging on now. From his deep stance, the younger man picked at Sifu's elbows, pressing him in the heavier, grinding, double-handed style. Sifu followed without losing balance. The stranger grew bolder in confidence; his sweeping matriculations began buffeting the old man in close.

Sifu continued to counter, but his defensive changes grew smaller and smaller. Inexorably, he was being worn away by the brilliant stranger who pressed the old man into ever greater constrictions of space. The silence was oppressive and the pressure was palpable in the room. It was no longer a matter of why our old master would not strike back; he was on his heels, period, fighting for his dignity and dead in the younger man's sights. His power assured, his mastery complete, the water-boxer struck at Sifu with startling finesse—thumping shoulder strikes against the old man, toying with him like a cat with its prey. It was all but over; gloom settled over the watching students. All that remained, it seemed, was the way in which the final stroke would be played out.

It came in a storm, in one of the lulls that settle in during push-hand sessions when the thigh muscles begin to scream for relief. One moment Sifu rocked forward in his old, slight way, the very next the stranger had withdrawn, coiled like a snake, rocketing upward dead at Sifu's breast-center line. The attack was a blur, a sure-fire direct hit; there was no resisting.

Crash! It was over. Faster than lightning, than thought or sight, a body flew through the air, crashing hard on its shoulder with a tremendous leaden thud. *Wham!*

Our eyes opened wide in amazement. Master Ng stood laughing uproariously. Ten feet away in a heap, the stranger battled to shake out the cobwebs. Tom, the instigator of it all, fell in a pall, his face drained of color as Chung suggested softly to him, "You better go now."

Wayman, a quiet boy who spoke the best English among the Chinese students, approached Errol and me. "This is Sifu's Cool-Heart Tai Chi," he said plainly. "Now maybe you can understand when Sifu says 'Critical Moment.' It's not easy to put in words."

Sifu began turning out the lights. I helped him with his coat and he gave me a look.

"Wu-wei," he said, nodding his head lightly up and down, lips drawn in tight in the Cantonese way, indicating a hard lesson or close shave with the reaper. His eyes were dancing; there was victory in them somewhere maybe, but mostly I just saw brightness.

"Tao," he said with a small click of his head, thumbs up for emphasis. We were leaving now with the others. "Tao *very big*!"

Strangely, he was almost whispering. No crowing about him. Keeping it secret between us. "Don't you think too much, Mr. Trevor. . . . Only *do*! Tao no can lose!"

20

ON MASTERY

S OTO ZEN MASTER DOGEN writes somewhere that it is not so much the ideals of Zen that are worth mastering as its methods of self-discipline. His deep insight is equally applicable to Tai Chi.

In *Treasury of the True Dharma Eye,* a collection of his writings, Dogen offers a trenchant understanding of the thought, conduct, and sensory awareness appropriate to followers of the Buddha dharma—what iron-shirt Taoists might call *the Way.* The models and examples Dogen offers us are Mountains. He notes:

"As for mountains, there are mountains hidden in jewels; there are mountains hidden in marshes, mountains hidden in the sky; there are mountains hidden in mountains. There is a study of mountains hidden in hiddenness" (translated by Carl Bielefeldt).

There is a study of mountains hidden in hiddenness: What are we to make of an idea like this? Replace the word "mountain" with "master" and it seems monumental, for they are interchangeable. Dogen adds further, "Therefore we should thoroughly study these mountains. When we thoroughly study the mountains, this is the mountain training. Such mountains and rivers themselves spontaneously become wise men and sages."

Dogen's understanding and self-discipline are not that of the drill sergeant. Rather, they specifically discuss what is better understood as sacred teaching. Dogen teaches us that the true master is the Mountain and that the Mountain is the Buddha, and that we acquire this understanding only by being in the presence of masters. To know a real path—Tai Chi or whatever else it might be—and to truly practice it means to live it; there is no either-or. Anything else can be valued accordingly. We must choose our models well.

Sacred teaching is learned by rote, by repetitive exercise with good reason. One is that it is usually more subtle and difficult to master than it seems. Another is that successive generations must regenerate the sacredness of the teaching for themselves. Fulfillment in discipline of this nature comes from honoring the tradition, in acquiring the learning as it has been set down. In the case of Tai Chi, like Zazen, it must be practiced regularly and faithfully to derive any benefit.

Ultimately, every seeker must embrace his or her own vision of the teaching and dance his or her own dance. It has been this way ever since Lao-tzu explained that no one could know his Tao. Tao is Tao, but each of us brings our own something to absolute reality. The big picture is there *everywhere,* but its intrinsic nature remains unknowable and unnameable. Taoism begins and rests with this very ambiguity.

Tai Chi's circle of perfection lies within the rigor of self-discipline, of mindful everyday practice of our *practice.* The challenge as a student of Tai Chi, of the Tao, is to bring this rhythmic energy, chi, to realization. The oversight of the first wave of Western Zen and East-West culture enthusiasts in the 1950s and 1960s was its neglect of the basic Asian example by which self-realization is achieved: *practice.* Practice means following a regular path. A true path is learned only sketchily from books; it requires a teacher. Acquiring mastery ourselves involves acquiescing to the example of one knowledgeable in the path we wish to tread. So long as it is free of abusive or exploitative means, in agreeing to follow the teacher's example, we offer our tacit approval of the instruction he or she employs. In essence, we submit.

Submission is problematic for Westerners. It is hard to call another "master." The West's is a highly individualistic civilization; from our early years we are educated to cherish the self and never to surrender it, even on pain of annihilation. Spiritual submission, however, does not involve "surrender." We can view it as an alchemical reaction in the way that sand submits to the potter in order to become an urn, or how gold submits to the forge to emerge as a chalice.

The most comical part of the process is the discovery of how effortless the correct path really is. What hard work we go through to achieve what is really only a small and simple reward! Enlightenment, after all, is no big thing; the real challenge, as three thousand years of mystics remind us, lies in simple everyday living. The reward, however, is astonishing: The Great Jewel of Thankfulness. If we are fortunate enough to find a real teacher, one who is in it for the long haul, we come to realize it is not the master who will leave us; always it is the student who leaves in time. The true master remains always with us, within us. This is the real meaning of mastery; it is a synonym for *love*. This is what Dogen understood.

The Master Is Always There. This is fundamental. In the sincerest form of meditation, for the briefest flicker when form and motion cease, our master appears in affirmation. The master's own spirit moves within us as a prelude to the dissolution of all dharmas, all teachings. This is Master Dogen's teaching of how sacred transmission is effected; when "practice and verification are nonexistent," then we have achieved the highest moment of our practice, and in echo of another great Zen master, Hakuin, we may truly

> *Enter the forest without moving the grass;*
> *Enter the water without raising a ripple. . . .*

21

Down Inna Babylon

THE OLD ROCKER CAPTAIN Beefheart has this gutsy tune: "I have to run so far to find a Clear Spot." Tai Chi people know exactly what he means.

During my first five years of training, I exercised mornings in a quiet courtyard between two aging apartment buildings. In warm weather, a tall hawthorn kept it shady; during the rainy season a quiet, paved corner offered safe footing. It was a secluded spot and my early-morning presence there went more or less unnoticed.

During heavy rain, my apartment living room was just large enough to permit my working through a full three-set routine. Nothing compares with Tai Chi practice outdoors though, and a regular place to play is essential for any serious development. It helps a lot if your living space affords a little privacy.

Unlike in Asia, Tai Chi—or for that matter any meditative practice—is still a relatively uncommon public sight in North America. I've learned that it's just as well to try to establish a clear spot of our own somewhere. This was brought home to me once when I visited an artist friend on an island north of the Olympic Peninsula.

Tomas lived above the high-tide mark on a sweeping volcanic shoulder above the water with neighboring homes stretching along the rugged shorefront. There for a long weekend, one sunny morning I borrowed a fishing pole before the others arose and went out to throw a line with the hope of catching breakfast. It was an especially fine time of day. The line sank deep near a kelp bed and I waited.

I was barefoot and the gritty, pumicelike surface of the hardpan ridge felt good beneath my feet. Securing the butt of my pole in a cleft of rock, I began a few stationary limbering-up exercises. The ridge sloped to the sea, but it seemed worth a try and I began to move, feeling my way about the ground. Ten or twelve minutes later, sometime during the third set—*White Stork Spreads Its Wings*—I noticed my rod tip jerking like crazy.

Back in the kitchen, I gutted the fat greenling. It was large enough to feed six or seven. My wife was rummaging through the cupboards in search of ginger or a few condiments when Tomas came in from his studio.

"That was some war hula you were up to out there, mister," he said, giving the clean fish a once-over. "Looks like it worked to boot."

"It ain't always like that. Just a lucky day, but it feels good." I looked at my wife, Kwangshik, smiling.

"Some of the neighbors around will be wondering what you were up to out there, I reckon," Tom continued. "I saw a couple of 'em giving you the Stranger Eye from their deck. We're a pretty claustrophobic bunch on the island here. You know how it is with anything new; although I must admit it did look vaguely intimidating, menacing."

Intimidating, menacing. I made note of these operative words. In any sort of public situation, the unfamiliar may provoke unpredictable reactions. Even bears are startled when puny humans blunder into their territory unannounced—*ding-dong*! Reaction can be unpredictable. It is best, one learns, to put some space around ourselves outdoors if we can.

It was about this time that a prominent entertainment magazine I wrote for was organizing its annual Las Vegas junket for big advertising customers. The plotline for this three-day idyll in Babylon was basic: charter a plane, fill it with dependable revenue producers and their escorts, zip 'em to the Neon City That Never Sleeps, bunk 'em, booze 'em, wow 'em, and sign 'em up on the way home for the next fifty-two-week advertising contract with the mag. To spice up the fare, selected writers, media freeloaders, and "special celebrity guests" were also fetched for laughs en route.

We stayed at the old Frontier Hotel on the Strip, a comfortable place from an older time in Vegas, and at least as gaudy as anything else on the Strip where something as inoffensive as buying yogurt can seem a subversive, possibly un-American act.

I'd been on the junket the previous year and, horrified at the Babylonian excess, had devised a unique solution. Rising early each morning, I drove my rented compact out into the desert. With a couple of large, white towels, a thermos of cold water, and a bag of washed fruit, I'd find a drivable rise off the road somewhere, turn off, and unload. Spreading the towels to sit in comfort—and picking out unfamiliar desert critters that might approach with the view of snacking on my hide—I'd cover my head and sit zazen meditation through the day, spelling off with reading and walking meditation through the amazingly peaceful high-desert cactus and sage. A quick plunge in the frigid Colorado River mitigated any thermostat problems.

This year, however, my wife had joined the junket. Fond of games of chance, she'd found a welcome at the Frontier casino and a hard first-day's night there kept her abed next morning. It was a stunning summer's day to be outdoors early. I made my way out to the hotel's spacious garden and pool area where black-throated desert sparrows chirped high and sweet in the ornamental shrubbery. The recreational area was spacious, but cramped by row upon row of still-vacant deck chairs. Apparently, I was the only human being moving at that hour, but discretion urged me toward a clear spot and I spied a shady nook at the farther end of the patio.

Slipping off my flip-flops, I set up shop and began loosening my limbs. The patio was surrounded by the high walls and imposing dark glass of a nighttime convention center of some sort, so I enjoyed a kind of complete privacy even within such a popular visitor oasis.

A three-set round of Yang-style Tai Chi runs thirteen to twenty minutes, although it can run much longer or even a bit shorter, depending on one's disposition, inspiration, and whether or not there's a plane to catch. Throw in a ten-minute warm-up and a quarter of an hour of Tai Chi Sword and you're looking at forty-five minutes to an hour of practice each day. That's to go somewhere farther with Tai Chi. Most students, newcomers especially, typically invest about fifteen minutes a day, and this is all right too.

I was midway through the second set when the voice of authority rang out.

"Freeze!" it barked. "Hold it right there!"

I held it right there, flashing instantly that I was in Las Vegas—when I could have been sensibly far off in the desert.

The voice emerged into view on my right. A policeman in

drab brown uniform. A big man, a veteran; hand on his holster, no hat and thin water-slicked hair. He'd cocked his holster, but mercifully the gun was not drawn.

"Don't move."

"You've got my attention, officer," I said fretfully.

He very cautiously drew nearer. I read his uniform emblem: SECURITY. He was huge and, although aging, three times my size and bulk. He fairly inched toward me, his hand on the butt of what looked like Clint Eastwood's Colt .45.

"What's happening?" I asked. "I'm a registered guest in this hotel."

"What's going on out here?" he asked. "People are complaining about you *in there.*"

He nodded with his head toward the convention center. I had a good look at him now; he bore a cultivated resemblance to John Wayne. I also understood he was as unsure of me as I was frightened of him.

"Who's complaining about me?" I wanted to know. "I'm a guest here—with the Media Advertisers party—I haven't seen a soul anywhere this morning."

He ignored me.

"I want to talk to the manager about this," I demanded, adding my own emphasis on security.

"*Those* people in *there* are complaining about you," the guard shot back. "And they're complaining about *you* to the manager."

He pointed to the black wall again. "What the hell are you doing here, anyway? You from Vietnam?"

Some gambling fool had me pegged for a shell-shocked Vet. Or maybe Vegas just didn't dig unconventional guests. I relaxed a little, thinking it was simply a John Wayne vs. James Bond–type showdown.

"Just who are the mystery guests who are complaining?" I asked again. "I'd like to know."

"Those people right inside there!" Big John yelled. "Those people eating their breakfast; they don't wanna be staring at you doing your *Kay-rati,* or whatever it is, while they're eating."

Things were spinning out of control. There were no breakfasting Eurocentrics in sight. "Officer," I said quietly, "there's nobody there, just look. It's all black. Closed up tight."

"I *know* it's all black," he said. "*You can't see 'em 'cuz you ain't supposed to see 'em, mister.* That's a one-way mirror! They can see out, but you *can't* see in, get it? That's the Frontier Hotel's breakfast lounge and it's chock-full of guests sitting in there having to look at you half-naked out here, moving around, doing that hoodoo!"

Such moments are called *satori* in Zen parlance. Sudden awakening. Inwardly, I considered exciting new employment, something far, far away, possibly with Monty Python's Ministry of Silly Walks.

O Merciful Buddha!

Like the good Captain says, *I have to run so far to find a Clee-eer spot. . . .* Lao-tzu understood this all too well:

> *Therefore, the humble is the root of the noble*
> *Not putting on a display, we shine forth*
> *Not justifying ourselves, we are distinguished*
> *Not boasting, we receive recognition. . . .*
> (translated by Gia-Fu Feng and Jane English)

22
INNER-CITY EDEN

T O BUY OUR FIRST home, my wife and I found ourselves living in a part of Vancouver that town planners politely call a "transitional neighborhood." Life in a low-income district with a larger-than-average number of urban aggravations was a chance we took in exchange for living in, what in every other respect, was a beautiful location.

A funky little minipark up the road presented itself as a likely place to work out each morning. It hovered above a steep embankment overgrown by a bramble jungle only a spit above the harbor. Vancouver's north-shore mountains towered across the water.

In the eastern corner of the park, an enormous maple had been allowed to stand, its foliage blooming like an oasis of optimism, and I was reminded of how the Buddha found his enlightenment beneath just such a friendly bodhi tree. In season it would keep off either rain or heavy sun. Immediately adopting this lovely site as my new dharma home, I worked out daily beneath its heavy branches for the next five years.

Gradually, the beat-up little park came to life. A neighbor lady who walked her dog each day was the first to overcome her suspicion and say hello. Old Mr. Alexander, a Polish widower, began sharing gardening secrets. Once they'd seen a lo-fan out playing Tai Chi, Chinese newcomers who might otherwise have been unsure of the area began turning up mornings to exercise nearby as well. Residents from the large native aboriginal community nearby that gave the area its nickname of "the Reserve" took to hanging out in Tai Chi corner near the big tree as well, and kept it tidy. Increasingly, people picked up after their dogs; more often than not, bottles and litter were placed in the garbage can. Amid the everyday, inner-city blues of the east end, our tiny neighborhood space enjoyed a special dispensation. It stayed cheerful. People began calling it "Tai Chi Park."

One winter morning beneath the heavy old maple, I wrapped up my routine and wrote the following:

PLAYING TAI CHI IN THE SNOW

Ice crystals snap beneath my feet:
Grasp the Bird's Tail . . .
Bundle up thick against dawn chill,
Turn at the waist;
At four below zero nostrils sting on the in-breath.

Above, maple resonates—birdsong on December air:
Who'd think the starling such a virtuoso?
Pain-in-the-ass dogturds flick away frozen
Snap!
Arms and feet move in unison,
Uncoiling like an old, hot snake.
Mountains ring the bay, the span at Lion's Gate;
Gulls hover in shimmering light,
Ribbons of exhaust drift up the cliffs,
Richly vital.
World about its work:
Every moment alive.

Unbidden, I'd come up with my first Tai Chi poem. Another came not long afterward. It had to do with awareness, something I worked at every morning beneath the harbor maple.

Becoming aware and staying aware are like parallel railway lines; they head in the same direction, but each has its own story. Between the special moments of Big Awakening are many daily experiences that, at best, may be only small awakenings. These constitute the mainframe of any path to self-realization. Keeping at our practice requires a different level of commitment than most of us are used to. It means breaking the bad human habit of slacking off. No excuses accepted.

In one of the spells of rebellion that periodically afflict every follower of a path requiring constancy of practice, I struggled against the self-imposed obligation of slogging wearily to Chinatown come hell or high water. Of course, I went anyway. It was during one of these difficult evenings that I finally experienced a major breakthrough in refining a technique that had eluded me for months. I summarized it thus:

THE EIGHTFOLD PATH

Sometimes the weariness takes over:
All this rain; I'll never make the next dharma class. . . .
We drag ourselves along,
practice anyway; heavy bodied, moving slow.
Keep to your course, minor Buddha;
nearly there.
Keep to the course; so many others drift astray,
lost in the world.
Who else to keep the master's lantern burning?
There's nectar even in weary practice,
O Bodhisattva;
in rowing the dharma boat to farther shores,
clad even in our old fatigues.

Discipline, we learn through our aches and pains and smiles, is its own reward. The discipline of Tai Chi teaches us about being conscious in this very moment, without distraction, getting through the project to hand from movement to movement, with a crystalline focus on whatever it is we are doing. It's a good skill to have when you're perched high on a ladder fixing your old house in a hard-to-reach place, or backtracking a forest trail in the dark when you've stayed out too long with a friend who's getting nervous, or working in a dangerous environment with high-risk opponents all around you. The self-discipline of Tai Chi is about containment and release of energy at just the appropriate moment; or letting the river run and surfing the dynaflow. It's a skill that returns us to the very first garden. You can use it for poetry, or for keeping a good marriage alive. It's a skill you can acquire that might save your life.

23

HOLDING TO THE COURSE
WITH ALLEN GINSBERG

MY WIFE AND I had recently returned from a lengthy journey through Asia in May 1985 when the telephone rang one morning. The call came from Rex Weyler, a dharma writer at Hollyhock Farm on the fairly remote Cortes Island, in British Columbia.

"Can you come up here for a poetry workshop we're having with Allen Ginsberg this weekend?" he asked. "Someone's donated a scholarship and we'd like to offer it to you."

Two days later, I was waiting at the gantry bay of a small trunk airline with my bag, typewriter and Tai Chi sword in hand as a familiar-looking character shuffled down the corridor. A friend at the farm had said Allen would be flying on the 9:00 A.M. flight, too.

"Howdy."

"Hello."

"You're flying up to Cortes?" I inquired.

"Yeah. . . . You flying to Campbell River as well?"

"I don't live there," I said. "I'm ferrying on through to Holly-hock for the workshop with you. Welcome to the coast."

We stood talking a moment. Allen seemed tired but looked fine in a black leather jacket and khaki trousers. Steel-rimmed glasses, potbelly, grizzled beard. Easygoing.

We boarded the plane that had only fifteen or twenty passengers. Allen took a window seat up front and asked if I'd like to sit beside him. We buckled up and as the plane taxied and left the ground, I checked to see if he had any special reinforcements for takeoff—prayers, mudras, signs of the cross. None visible. We looked out the window, climbing. I pointed out the Cascade Range, the mighty Fraser River; then the delta lands, downtown Vancouver, the Indian reserve, Wreck Beach. . . .

"You really know your city," he said. "That's good. Not common. Do you know much about Cortes?"

"Hollyhock's evolved from the late sixties and early seventies," I explained.

"Originally, it was a sort of Esalen-North called Cold Mountain Institute. Alan Watts, Gary Snyder, Gregory Bateson—people like that used to visit."

"Gary's been there? Alan Watts, too?"

"Alan came a couple of times. It's an incredible place. I think you'll like it. Maybe you can just hang out for a while. How long do you have?"

"I've got five or six days."

We munched on Danish pastries. "What do you do?" Allen asked. There was an earnest generosity about him, like an interesting teacher.

"I'm a writer."

"What do you write?" He dunked some Danish in his juice. "Things that interest me mostly—Tai Chi, music, art, literature...."

"Tai Chi? I play Tai Chi," he said. I listened keenly.

"Maybe we can play together," I replied. "It's a large part of my life. Where'd you learn?"

"At Naropa. There are two people teaching there. Yang style from Taiwan."

"Any good?"

"I think so. They're from Cheng Man-ching's style. I haven't practiced as much as I should lately. Maybe at Cortes."

Early next morning the cool gulf waters glistened to the north. The soft tock of a hunting owl nearby during the night left me reflecting on its Indian symbolism as I chose a level spot near a clutch of trees on higher ground. Across the sound, the Beaufort Range peaked above the dawn mist. I took in lungfuls of the salty tang. Not too many gullies underfoot: it was an ideal place to exercise and breathe. I warmed up and began my routine. Partway through, Allen came walking up the rise from his beach house below, clad in his black leather coat again. I could see his gray-white beard and glasses glinting as he circled the path to the lodge ground. He walked toward an open area a respectful thirty yards distant, nodding in recognition without speaking.

Facing north, he began moving in black cotton kung fu shoes that I feared would get wet in the dewy grass. It seemed no hindrance. He played straightforwardly, occasionally misplacing a step or two, but working sufficiently well enough to account himself as a good determined learner. He stayed perhaps ten minutes, then left as silently as he'd arrived.

I continued through my set, then practiced with the sword. From the corner of my eye I traced a figure or two looking out from the lodge window, but put them aside and finished the ritual. Inside the lodge, I met Allen at breakfast. We chatted over our coffee and porridge about Tai Chi; how we'd come by it, about our teachers, Asia, and the like.

"You practice often?" he asked.

"Pretty much every day."

"That often?"

"That's the way we learn it. Like Zazen," I said, a little taken aback. "Something we do every day."

"That's good if you can keep it up," Allen said. He if anyone would understand the meaning of regular, mindful practice.

"You still have a teacher?" I inquired. He did. "He doesn't practice every day?" I asked.

"He probably does," Allen said. "I don't. I manage when I can . . . in my apartment mostly. Don't you get tired of it, practicing like that every day?"

It was the first time I'd ever considered the possibility. Illness, travel, unforgiving weather—these were tolerable excuses for skipping an occasional practice, I felt; at least in a pinch. Sifu's injunction for as long as I'd known him had been, "Practice every day."

"I'm a little surprised," I said to Allen. "I'd have thought you'd keep at it. . . . Like sitting every day."

He shrugged it off. "When you get to a certain level, I don't think you really have to do it *every* day," he surmised. "It's okay to knock off now and again, just so long as you keep at it. I think it'd become relentless otherwise."

At this point, other participants and organizers were catching Allen's attention and we took leave of each other, readying for business. I joined a small group with whom I'd be spending the day's proceedings and put the matter out of mind.

The retreat ended some days afterward and people went their separate ways. But an uneasiness lingered. For years, Allen's work had been important to me. I'd read his words and found great insight in them. Now, having met him, I'd been rattled by his laissez-faire approach to practice. Worse, I found myself slacking off and giving in to informality. The best solution seemed to be a discussion with my teacher, Sifu. Through one or two other students, I explained where I'd been recently and what Allen Ginsberg had made of Tai Chi self-discipline. Sifu only seemed confused and wanted to know who Mr. Ginsberg was.

My explanation that he was a prominent teacher and transmitter of East-West thought did little to clarify matters. Sifu just shook his head.

"Only practice," he said, before looking me in the eye. "Practice every day. This is Tai Chi."

I'd like to say that was the final word, but it wasn't. Somehow, meeting up with a Western teacher who'd been so important to me knocked me right out of the loop I'd been in for six long years. I monkeyed with Allen's advice for a while; it offered a little more freedom, more flexibility, but in the end I paid for it. Giving up on what in Sifu's group we called "iron-shirt" discipline also brought some pain: as the maxim says, "Having tasted stolen honey, you can't buy innocence for money."

Three or four months later, I worked out my jimjams and got back to daily practice. Tai Chi, I realized, if we employ it as a vehicle for growth, is more than an exercise. Like prayer, it's larger than a recreation: it is a contemplative tradition. As a meditative tradition based on certain patterns of physical activity and ability, Tai Chi's beautiful patterns need regular maintenance, or they fray. Additionally, to break through to higher levels of physically expressing real wu-wei *in action,* daily practice is irreplaceable.

Yet, every farmer understands the idea of leaving soil to fallow. Perhaps what Allen was really saying is that at a certain point, our practice begins permeating other aspects of our daily life. Perhaps it changes form for a spell. And anyway, Mr. Allen Ginsberg can't be expected to go into everything all the way: he saved his best for his poetry and activism. He'd be a different individual otherwise.

Allen's poetry retreat and his comprehensive knowledge of poetry and poetics were chastening in its depth and cohesion. His generosity was constant and unconditional. On the final afternoon, we took a group forest walk while Allen expounded on *The Diamond Sutra.* Poetry and writing are equally valuable forms of practice, he offered, suggesting the Sutra for further study reading. "Diamond signifies toughness, hardness," he said. "It could also mean Tough Teacher."

Allen's words come back to me often. Whatever our path—Tai Chi, Yoga, Buddhism, Christianity, playing the piano—we're either in it fully, or we're not.

"Lighten up, mate," the precious Muse still reminds me, from time to time. "Keep it soft."

24

MAKING THE SPIRIT SING

SIFU TELLS A STORY about Hau, his longtime student in Hong Kong. As a young man, Hau wanted to learn Tai Chi and pestered Master Ng for months in the hope of receiving instruction. Finally, Sifu relented.

"I showed him how to perform one movement only: *Cloudy Hands,*" Sifu says. "For four or five months, that was all. In the olden days, this is how my Sifu taught."

Hau balked at such instruction but was patient enough to stay the course. According to Master Ng, after endlessly repeating the same movement for five months, Hou acquired a good understanding not only of *Cloudy Hands,* but of the whole underlying approach to Tai Chi practice. Having shown sufficient willingness, he was then instructed into formal training. Sifu explains this classical method in terms of responsibility: if students in pre-Maoist China used their kung fu knowledge in the commission of a criminal act, their master was considered party to the action for having taught them and was therefore liable. Teachers were justifiably deliberate in how they paced a student's education.

I did not think of this when I first saw Sifu performing Tai Chi Sword one summer evening in Chinatown. Arriving early, I stumbled upon him teaching Mah something I'd never seen before. Holding a wooden pointer, Sifu snapped his heels as he wove a complex tapestry of movements that, while Tai Chi–related, were of another, higher order of accomplishment.

Some time after this, I saw Sifu playing sword out of doors. He practiced in a blue silk Chinese jacket, swaying as he rocked from posture to posture, swirling a fine chrome blade with a knotted tassel. It was pure, undefiled: similar to ritual Sufi dancing but with a flashing blade to hand. His movements spoke directly to the heart. I was held spellbound by their unearthly fullness. Like seeing Tai Chi for the first time again, but deeper this time, more holy, more profound. I wanted to learn.

But Sifu was in no rush to give of his knowledge. One Chinese student left in frustration for another teacher. "These old Taoists," he said between his teeth; "they never want to pass their information on." A new school in town, he informed us—a kind of franchise operation—taught students sword form after only six months of study. He was off to learn. We never saw him again.

The rest of us kept our counsel, never asking directly for the teaching. We assumed it would come, like all else, when Sifu thought we were ready. From time to time, we attempted to engage him in sword-related banter to no avail. Yet my interest persisted and grew as every Saturday and Sunday I watched Sifu execute the precision of the graceful sword form.

"Tai Chi Sword," he told us once. "The sword is all footwork. Without good Tai Chi first, you can't learn it. Sword takes a long, long time." Then he added, "In China we say, in sword form there are no friends."

During the third year of my Tai Chi training, on a magical mystery hike in the wilderness with a Tai Chi brother, I came upon a large rib bone. It looked frighteningly familiar, perhaps human, for we were near an ancient aboriginal site.

It was hot, and we'd hiked well beyond the last remote camp-sites on an arid, ranchland plateau overlooking a deep river canyon. We rested awhile in the shade of an acacia grove near one of the few creeks visible in the area, and I found the rib bone near a mound of scree. I played with the bone a little, then moved through a brief round of Tai Chi. A feeling I cannot describe came over me then, and I began to move in a different fashion, swaying and swooping the bone through the air. These move-ments took form and rhythm and I found myself raptured in a kind of frenzy, a dervish dance with the bone, swirling and scything in a way not unlike I'd seen Sifu do so often. Whether it was the heat, or some other phenomenon, I came out of the experience convinced that Sifu would recognize my desire and readiness to learn the sword form.

But it would take another twelve months, my fourth long year of training, before one bright July morning Sifu would pause and turn to me with his sword, showing me the center and beginning movements. Later, browsing in Chinatown, we found a wooden practice sword and I bought it for nineteen dollars. My study of sword form began as awkwardly as the ugly duckling's first summer in the pond.

Tai Chi Sword is a higher, more vibrant form of practice. One is in command of a weapon. It takes but a short time to understand what is meant by the admonition, "There are no friends in Tai Chi Sword"—like dancing among nettles.

As Sifu averred, in sword form, footwork *is* all. Furthermore, the expression of both mood and emotion is integral to sword form movement. Abstract ideas such as "happiness," "melancholy," and "spritely vigor" must be executed crisply, yet remain unforced. It is as awkward as learning the piano. Like the mother Tai Chi Chuan forms from which they derive, sword-work forms are gifted with elegant titles and a glance at them reveals the poetry of Tai Chi philosophy and practice: *Shower Overhead, Rhinoceros Gazes at the Moon, Wind Overturns the Lotus Leaves, Dragonfly Flits upon the Water, Grand Preceptor Picks Up Sword. . . .*

One learns that Tai Chi Sword is an aesthetic in itself, and that just as the *Tao Te Ching* inspires one to progress logically on to study other works of inspiration and instruction, so sword form compels us to seek good text advice. Sun-tzu's *The Art of War* is the obvious leap of imagination here; however, sword-minded practitioners will find there is nothing better than the Japanese Master Miyamoto Musashi's *Book of Five Rings*. Obviously, there are differences—the Japanese sword has its own unique structural genius—but the *thought*, the flowering visualization Musashi brings to the whole conceptualization of "Sword-Mind," is incomparable.

After a year of dedicated sword practice, I was again guided by Sifu through the mysterious tangle of shops in Chinatown. He'd heard of a fine blade that was up for sale, he said. We scouted it out: a flawless, chromed blade with leather sheath and dragon tassels trimmed in green Taoist knot-work. Sifu appraised it carefully: "Good one," he said quietly. "This okay, I think. You like?"

I was fascinated by the object. *A sword.* Sifu had spoken many times of the spirit a good sword possesses. To succeed in sword practice is known as "making the spirit sing." Next morning, I grasped the blade softly in my hands with exquisite pleasure. The real thing. Its weight brought a certainty and acuity to my practice. Gliding and swirling, scything and snapping, the spirit of the sword sang in my hand as the grass brushed like velvet beneath my feet. Though it is mannerly and retains Tai Chi's softness, ideally the sword form is conducted with businesslike efficiency while remaining outwardly gentle.

Meanwhile, red-breasted robins, unalarmed, hunted worms not far away. Nearing completion and returning to the still point, I heard a flourish of robin song thrill the summer air. Something, I understood, was working *just so.*

How could one resist? And so, I began again, stepping—almost floating—in silence, with the sword flitting as briskly as a bird in a thicket. It was, I sensed clearly, the very closest a human comes to flying.

25

TAI CHI SWORD: SEQUENCE OF MOVEMENTS

T HE POETRY OF TAI CHI Sword's sequence of movements is exquisite. In part, this is an homage to the literature that is central to China's root cultural philosophy, and which served as the educational syllabus in the development of its ruling civil service class of literary scholars that flourished for almost two thousand years. For Confucius, the moral arbiter of Chinese civilization, poetry was an adjunct of music. Traditionally it was intended to be sung, and music was the conceptual adjunct of the formal rites and ceremonies that gave the passage of days and seasons purpose and rhythm. In this sense, poetic movement expresses the fuller joys of existence.

Because the sequence of sword forms has been rarely recorded in a published English translation, it is presented here as supplementary material. Notice in the flow of gestures what sense of rhythm accompanies each body movement and the variety of ways in which it is expressed through animal form—through dragon, phoenix, honeybees, swallows, leaping horses and fish, herons, eagles, and tigers. Each has its own deliberate pace and nuance of form. Observe how minute particulars of nature lend name to various sword postures and strikes—the transient, drifting beauty of snowflakes and spring blossoms; the spotless purity of the lotus, or the profound illumination of the moon—perennially associated in the Far East with sadness and longing. There is the agricultural laborer's scything of the hay while searching for snakes, the busy housekeeper's dusting with a broom: indeed, from the aesthetic to the mundane, everything becomes one in the vivid impression resonance and vitality of sword form.

1. *Beginning*
2. *Step and Turn*
3. *Great Preceptor Points the Way*
4–5. *Three Rings Around the Moon*
6. *Grand Suppressing Star*
7. *Swallow Skims the Water*
8. *Sweep to the Right*
9. *Sweep Broom to the Left*
10. *Sweep Broom to the Right*
11. *Small Suppressing Star*
12. *Yellow Bee Darts in the Hole*
13. *Attentive Cat Catches the Mouse*
14. *Swirling Wind Sword*

15. *Dragonfly Flits on the Water*
16. *Swallow Darts to the Nest*
17. *Phoenix Spreads His Wings*
18. *Small Suppressing Star*
19. *Snowflakes Shower Over the Head*
20. *Swirling Wind, Left*
21. *Swirling Wind, Right*
22. *Searching for Snakes in the Grass*
23. *Embrace the Moon*
24. *Sending Birds to the Woods*
25. *Black Dragon Waves His Tail*
26. *Wind Overturns the Lotus Leaves*
27. *Tiger Covers the Head*
28. *Step Back with Three Strokes of the Sword*
29. *Turn About and Rein in the Horse*
30. *Sweep the Feet Thrice*
31. *White Horse Leaps the Ditch*
32. *Trail the Sword and Turn About*
33. *Sea Spirit Watches the Water*
34. *Compass Needle*
35. *Flying Stars Chase the Moon*
36. *Rhinoceros Gazes at the Moon*
37. *Open Window to Gaze at the Moon*
38. *Turn and Catch the Moon*

39. *Stab with Sword Twice*
40. *Eagle Spreads Its Wings*
41. *Wave the Sword Left*
42. *Wave the Sword Right*
43. *Shoot the Arrow at the White Goose*
44. *White Ape Proffers Fruit*
45. *Flower Petals Fall*
46. *Maiden Weaves at Her Shuttle*
47. *Fish Leaps over the Dragon Gate*
48. *Turn About and Chop the Sword*
49. *Step Left Foot over the Fence*
50. *Step Right Foot over the Fence*
51. *Wind Blows Through the Plum Blossoms*
52. *Receive the Sword Through the Window*
53. *Dragon Spits the Pearls*
54. *Black Dragon Twists the Post*
55. *Catch the Moon at Bottom of the Sea*
56. *White Tiger Waves His Tail*
57. *Old Tree Spreads Strong Roots*
58. *Heron Flies Through the Clouds*
59. *Dragon Stretches Out His Claws*
60. *Great Preceptor Picks Up the Fruit*
61. *Clean the Duster in the Wind*
62. *Hands Hold the Tablet*
63. *Embrace the Sword and Close*

26

CLOUDY HANDS

CLAUDE, A TAI CHI friend, and I were strolling on a winter's day along the harbor seawall near English Bay. Moving west toward Kitsilano Point, we rounded the long bend in the pathway by the planetarium. The sun was deeply set, and the cloud formations above the bay glowed with a peculiar heaviness. Progressing along a wooded expanse of shorefront, I noticed a fantastic sight up in the sky, a perfectly formed Tai Chi warrior in the clouds. He was large and set off quite alone above Spanish Banks in the Crouching Tiger style.

The dimming sun burned ember-red around the figure, striated loosely here and there with gray and blackish daubs of vapor. Sitting in the left-leg stance, left hand coiled at hip, his right leg extended outward from the heel; the fighter's right arm and open hand skirmished forward, everything primed softly and economically in defensive readiness. Burning with energy, he radiated intense *keng,* or muscular strength—an emanation so powerful it was apparent even to Claude. Stepping aside to the margins of the wood, I took my lead from the cloudy teacher, duplicating his position, following it through logically and balancing both the left and right hands' striking and sweeping efforts. From his effortless, ready stance, the cloudy warrior's example mutated variously into either offensive or further defensive movement. It was an astonishing vision, an indelible mark in memory.

Claude and I walked on together as the cloud dancer held his position. Gradually, the sky beneath turned feathery blue. Inevitably, in the way of all white clouds, he shifted his form several times, as if clarifying his movement further until, ultimately— in homage to the fleeting nature of this dusty world—through his changes he dissolved entirely, becoming pure translucent vapor once more.

We stood watching the last of the transformations above us, silently, two good friends together.

"In France, when something like this happens, we say it's a song from the soul," Claude mused. "From the elegant universe, like when Piaf used to sing."

"Science says it's just molecules," I grinned skeptically as we resumed our walk.

"Ridiculous!" Claude scoffed with a Gallic shrug. "Anyone can see it's pure magic."

27

Down by the Bay

I LIVE WITH MY family at the edge of the rain forest where the Pacific coastal mountains meet the sea. Each morning, the reality of what wilderness means surrounds me as I play Tai Chi. A hundred feet away, western hemlock, red cedar, and fir take over. It's dark in there and it doesn't stop until the Arctic tree line fifteen hundred miles to the north. It's where the wild things dwell.

I am writing this by the bay in late January. The ground is frost-covered; the peaks of Buntzen and Eagle Ridge across the inlet are veined with snow. Thirty minutes ago, playing Tai Chi as the sun began showing over the mountains, I turned and saw a coyote haunched and scratching in the first weak rays of sunlight. I sensed he was male as he camped in a hollow near heavy brush beside a rushing creek. It was his color that stopped my breath: foxy red mottled with amber, with the sharp coyote ears, lean ribs, heavy winter coat. Remarkably beautiful. I gazed, only watching, moving slowly as can be: don't change the rhythm.

The dog of all dogs. Of course, I wanted him. I turned again and he was gone.

Walking back to the house for a thermos and pencil, I told my young son what I'd seen.

"That figures," he said. "We call it the Buddha Creek, don't we?"

Already, the coyote has indelibly entered my mind. Sitting here beside the bay making notes, shivering a little, I know he does not belong at my feet but in the real-time dreamworld of the wilderness, like the cormorant that floats on a butt end of driftwood, hanging his wings to dry.

Tai Chi brings so much together. I noticed this morning how my mind was chattering as I exercised, flitting from one random thought to another the way bushtits flock to a shrubbery and never stop rustling. Fix on the hand. Return to stillness, to the one thing. Then, a glimpse of shimmering watery calm. Absorption into the Big Picture. Tao. This is what Chang San-feng understood, the need to slow down, as the Buddha Shakyamuni learned before him.

Slowing down. People sometimes come up in the village coffee shop asking, "What was that you were doing in the park earlier? How come you move so slowly?"

Would it do to tell a stranger that without slowness there's only more chatter? About moving slowly when the nose picks up the faint, still-lingering scent of the skunks that hunt bushrats along the rocky, nighttime shore nearby? About herons, glimpsed from the corner of an eye on secluded shoals, taking pointers from them on form, balance? About a magic coyote?

Let's say it's just easier to mumble something about exercise, or morning backache, or meditation. And smile.

Always, unbidden, Tai Chi brings us messages from the Tao. Sixty feet away, paddling on the bay, a female goldeneye, a young duck, squawks at me, telling me something important.

Fix on the palm of your hand, mister. Keep moving. Don't think too much. Return to stillness.

28

WRECK BEACH MEDITATION

ABOUT THE TIME I began my training with Sifu, I took to spending more time in the woods and along the shoreline. During the warmer months especially, I found playing Tai Chi naked on the great sandbars of Vancouver's untamed Wreck Beach a special pleasure.

Wreck Beach stretches several miles along the foot of Vancouver's Point Grey bluffs. The rugged beach with its litter of huge drift logs and gnarled tree roots shunts abruptly against the steep, wooded cliffs that are home to many birds and small mammals. Bald eagles nest in the highest, remote cedars and summer kingfishers swoop the alders, punctuating the sea air with their steady characteristic rattle.

It is the great blue herons I find most precious. The opportunity of studying these large, elegant birds has always seemed to me a special gift. The Tai Chi dance, its calmness and tranquillity are derived from the heron, or at least its near cousin the white crane. To understand Tai Chi fully is to go and observe it

214 · *Trevor Carolan*

at its very source. Vancouver's own Chief Dan George writes of how aboriginal elders insisted young people study the heron to learn and master the art of patience in hunting. One late summer evening I made note of the following:

The evening tide creeps high as the heron flies in, unexpected. We have drifted off in love, in thought, or a book. Then a hush stills the bush; gulls flit hurriedly away across the sand: the heron swoops, circling to land upon a heavy rock surrounded by water. Breaking speed with foreshortened wing strokes, her pinfeathers prime the air. Gracefully she descends upon the island boulder.

The majestic bird preens a moment then cocks to attention, breast strikingly pale and blue-tinged against the dark of her silvery, streamlined torso. Great blue heron.

Every culture adopts this bird of stillness as its symbol of happiness. Egyptians revere the sacred ibis of the Nile. Throughout the Orient, *Tsurumi* is the bird of happiness and conjugal felicity. Celts and Europeans know chimney-dwelling storks as the bringers of new babies into the world. Ice Age man carved stalking herons onto woolly mammoth tusks. Why?

This is the largest bird most of us will ever see. Top predator, magnificent in flight. In spring, along the river marshes, the heron's courtship rite is so elaborate in nature that humans themselves came to copy it, creating a sacred dance, a ritual holy and particular to every culture, each in its own way. So too, evolved *Tai Chi,* the sacred dance of Mother China, its meditative richness.

The Wreck Beach heron leaps down, an ungainly sort of flop, yet with not a shred of energy misplaced. Now she wades on wiry bamboo stilts, purposefully, elegantly, to a sandy point among a few large stones, then sets, standing tall—rigidly at first, settling her long, tubed neck alertly at a forty-five-degree angle.

She waits perfectly, stiff-necked. The water laps about her legs. One, then two effortless, measured steps in the shallows. Rapidly, delicately, she bobs before striking. Hunched low, crooking reverse-knee joints, her drainpipe neck curves slowly, softly, then she flashes: *Needle to Sea Bottom.* The killing stroke. Her head emerges with a silvery smelt wriggling frantically in her beak. She flips it upward, acrobatically, slips it artfully down her gullet. A small crowd forms. The heron wades, fishing, no more than eight or ten feet from shore, almost directly in front of the stump where we camp. We are speechless, rapt as the handsome bird wades and strikes, flashing her ivory neck, gulping fish for her brood far above.

Passersby stand and marvel as our yellow-eyed stranger of the black stilt legs strikes again and again, retrieving prey. Throughout her hunting she scarcely creates a ripple or sound. Seldom do her lightning thrusts go awry. Her motions are calm and precise; there is precision in each thing she does, always economical. Her body itself is superbly symmetrical, wonderfully lean. She moves imperceptibly. We scarcely notice the changes.

Then, a loose hound barks up the beach. The heron whips about, crooking neck, striding nimbly among barnacled rocks.

Startled, she rises with a whirring heave, upward in a rising arc. We hear her cry out with a hard *Caw!* like a raven. She cries several times, flying off like a prehistoric creature oblique against the fading light above the sand flats. A single bird trailing long stilt feet behind, dissecting sky, neck curved, tucked inward, drawing legs into body, long and dark, wings spread Stuka-bomber-like with great, easy drafts of energy propelling her upward.

In my mind's eye, I see old Sifu crouch, bobbing downward at the knees, hands raised protectively, bent at elbow, crooked soft at wrist. Stepping forward on right foot, body sinking briskly, turning softly, right hand raised, striking at shadows, dancing, whirring effortless by with a tiny, dragon's hiss. *White Stork Spreads Its Wings, Needle to Sea Bottom, Fan Through the Back* . . . Chinese gestures of the heron dance.

The heron rises aloft, ever higher. For a time, a flock of gulls heckles her, trying to dodge off with a fish from her beak. They twitter and flap, my wife says, like Japanese ladies all afuss. Then the last we see: a great bird at great height flying northeast well above Wreck Beach cliffs, high above earth and weathered slopes, high above the gardens of Point Grey, past the farthest point in sight, flying off toward the mountains and the harbor, toward the mighty cedars.

The gate to all mystery.

29
THIS DEWDROP WORLD

O CCASIONALLY, THROUGH THE YEARS at dim sum, or while drinking tea with Sifu, I might glance at him to find his attention fixed elsewhere, remotely beyond the temporal world. At these moments, he was unusually serene, and once I wrote a note on the corner of a napkin: "Saw the old man acclimatizing himself to Death. It did not seem a fearful prospect to himl. . . . Transcendent."

Other aging people I've known lived in dread of death. It could not be mentioned in their presence, yet they were drawn toward it like a moth to a flame, constantly reading obituaries and attending funerals. When I intimated my thoughts on Sifu's faraway spells to Pang Yi, the painter, she said, "Don't be concerned. You don't know these old Chinese masters. Sifu will live a long time."

Once, when a beloved uncle of mine passed away, I asked Sifu what happens when we die. He explained it carefully, matter-of-factly in considerable detail: a traditional Chinese Taoist-Buddhist interpretation familiar throughout Asia in its series of Sevens:

seven days of mourning and grief in which the departed spirit wanders in need of reassurance, uncertain of what has happened; then fourteen days of memorial observance; next, twenty-one days, and so forth up to "Seven Sevens"—the auspicious forty-ninth day at which time the deceased's wandering soul may enter again into a new life-form or meet its appointed destination.

While Sifu's answer unfolded, I realized how little preparation modern secular life offers us as adults for this inevitable occasion. Then the phone rang one Monday morning.

Sifu's son-in-law, his onetime interpreter and by now my old friend, informed me somberly that during the night Sifu had experienced a severe stroke. He lay in the hospital in grave condition.

In my mind's eye, I saw the Indian summer morning the day previous. Sifu had sparred with five of us, one after the other, pushing hands and testing each. At ninety years of age, he had shadowboxed with five healthy men in their prime. It was almost unbelievable: we'd been doing it so long, the thought of overexertion had never occurred to any of us.

The news was devastating. And so began a phone-tree: Sifu was near death; he was not expected to survive. I realized how deeply my attachment had grown. Sifu was more than a teacher; he was my spiritual grandfather. Explaining all this to my wife, I readied for the hospital. Then, as I was dialing the phone to cancel work for that morning, it hit me: something like a voice. Go to your work, it said. Fulfill your responsibility to others first, then go and express your grief. It was Sifu talking. That was his way. Fulfill your responsibilities. See your duty through as a good citizen; be a good family man, a good student. Be a good teacher to your own students. Remember them first. The Bodhisattva Path.

After work that afternoon, feeling a tangle of emotions, I parked my car near the imposing pile of the city hospital and trudged uphill. Sifu lay unconscious in his room, attended by his elderly wife and daughter. Their grief was stark and overpowering. My precious teacher lay there, now looking his full ninety years at last, helpless and terribly frail. One side of his forehead was a frightful blue where fine bleeding had percolated through the tissues. His breathing was near invisible.

Si-heng Doug looked on. Quietly, he advised me of Sifu's condition. We suggested the ladies might benefit from a short break for tea: they were shattered and had been there all night. When they'd left I looked at Doug. "It's bad," he said. I agreed. We stood on either side of Sifu's bed among drips, catheters, and electronic monitors.

"It can't do any harm," I proposed. Together, gingerly, we took Sifu's bruised limbs in our hands and began Chi Kung vibration, softly, almost unnoticeably, treating the old man the way he'd healed us so many times throughout the years.

In Chi Kung healing, we attune to the circulation of our own inner chi and gently begin its transmission into the ailing other. As Sifu's family returned, they looked on, saying nothing. Simo understood. Off and on, Doug and I stayed at it into the night. The next day, we stayed at it for another eight or nine hours. Other visitors were coming all the time, of course, and Sifu's family were constantly with him. Doug and I worked out a schedule. One of us was there every day.

Slowly, day by weary day, matters came together. Sifu began to pull around. His eyes opened wide, he took liquids, began eating a little. Simo slept in a chair beside him; he was never alone. Little by little, the family and Doug could explain to him what had happened. Over and over, we practiced Chi Kung. It was entirely presumptuous on our part: Sifu had never formally acknowledged our abilities. We hoped he would not mind since he was still, more or less, unable to speak.

"How do you learn Chi Kung?" my wife had asked innocently one time.

Sifu had looked at her, incredulous, bemused. "Play a long time," he said, smiling instructively. "Do you have two or three years, twenty-four hours a day?" He explained how he lived with his master in China, night and day. "The chi can come anytime," he advised. "When you have lots of time, you can talk about it and learn."

His fifth day in the hospital, Sifu rested on his back, asleep.

Tests had determined his left side was partly paralyzed from the effects of the stroke. Gradually, he woke and tried to speak. Simo helped him with a straw and he drank a little clear juice. I stood opposite, by the bedside. Then, amazingly, Sifu, sallow and very ill, raised up his right arm. He raised his hand and I touched it with my fingers. Feebly, his hand began moving in a minuscule circle. Sifu was pushing hands—moving the chi. Simo's weary visage looked on, beaming in comprehension. I stayed with his hand in its movements.

"Toy-shou. . . . Push-hands," I said in Chinese. Simo wagged her head as a nurse came in. The nurse was dumbfounded at the sight—a ninety-year-old on his deathbed playing a hand game.

After this, it circulated through the wards that an unusual old man, Chinese, was healing himself in his room up the corridor. Two days later, Sifu sat up; then shuffled briefly, very weakly, with a walker in the hall. As his students, we escorted Sifu like gymnastic spotters. This first week of my master's illness was transformational in many ways, cementing our relationship at a different metabolic level. From the awkwardness of fumbling with urine bottles to helping with spoon feeding at dinnertimes, there wasn't much left unexplored in the visceral realm.

The doctors suggested it was time for an old folks' home.

"You don't understand," Sifu's supporters explained.

Four weeks later, Sifu returned home to his own bed. Simo

had stayed by his side all the while. No one knew what effect the illness would have on us all who followed his teaching. Without Sifu as leader, it seemed natural for things to fall apart. But this was Chinatown. We held together, bound in spirit, and kept meeting on Sundays, practicing as we were taught. Elder students led the group.

One morning the following spring, Sifu turned up unannounced. Someone brought him by car. We were lining up to play Tai Chi on the courtyard, perhaps a dozen of us, when a voice called out softly, *"Jo-San! Jo-San!* Morning!" Sifu was back like James Brown.

We played our set and Sifu wandered with his walking cane, quietly making suggestions here and there to improve a student's technique. Doug and I led up front; turning at one point—*Grasp the Bird's Tail*—and in keeping a general weather-eye on the old man, we caught a memorable glimpse of old Sifu across the grounds. He'd rambled off with one or two children and was gleefully bobbing a red balloon on a string. At the age of ninety, he was enjoying the privilege of being a kid once again.

Some months later, with Simo unwell from a heavy bronchitis, Sifu called on the phone and invited me over. When I arrived, the expectation was obvious. Sifu helped arrange a sitting chair for his wife. As Simo sat down, now grown rather frail, Sifu joined her by the edge of the couch.

Standing behind Simo, I tuned in with a silent meditation to help initiate the flow. With the process clear in mind, I commenced the internal massage along the meridians and pathways of Simo's back and arms. The Chi Kung that my master had taught me.

"The chi moves from our heart," Sifu taught. "Tai Chi . . . Chi Kung—same, same." When our heart is soft, then the chi can come; from our mind and heart, it can travel into another person.

Sifu looked on. I was treating his wife. My fingers moved, ranging over Simo's back the way I'd seen Sifu do on so many occasions. We spoke little, and then very quietly. When Chi Kung hands are soft, it is similar to push-hands; they detect where resistance or vulnerability lies. The hands trace the web of the body's musculature, noting zones of any irregularity—hardness, coldness, whatever it is that draws our energy and attention toward it.

I had practiced Chi Kung on my wife and parents, on family members and close friends for some years. From the first time I had seen him perform it on his patients, I was absorbed by its intensity; was drawn magnetically toward it. I had studied under Sifu's guidance and now explained what I noted in Simo's rhythms, the hindrances in circulation that were manifest to the fingertips. At other times, Sifu had corrected my touch or made adjustments when I'd practiced in his presence—on a student, or with one of the senior women who had adopted themselves into

Sifu's clan. A close friend sick with cancer had given me greater call to practice and, drained by the corrosive nature of his disease, I'd begun to understand the need for ever greater sensitivity in the Chi Kung handwork. Now I was being asked to practice on my master's own beloved wife. This time, Sifu made no corrections. He explained to Simo in Chinese what I'd told him. She replied sleepily, overcome with the drowsiness that is trademark in Chi Kung treatment.

"Simo says now your hands have kung fu. That's good," Sifu said. We continued in this way for several more days and Simo gradually improved.

After twelve years, my old master had signed his approval on what I could now do for others, as he'd done himself for the past fifty years. The occasion itself was remarkably calm. Sifu expressed his assent in true Taoist spirit: without ceremony or display, in silent confirmation.

It came simply, with the presentation of tea and an orange that he'd peeled, then we chatted together with Simo. Dharma transmission, they call it in Zen.

Naturally, there is no diploma.

Postscript

DURING THE WRITING OF this book Sifu Ng passed away quietly at the age of ninety-eight. I had visited him several days before and we talked a little about Tai Chi, but he had grown very weary. Ironically, Kuen—his oldest student from Hong Kong, an elder Tai Chi brother now himself in his seventies whom we had long heard of—was visiting at the time. It was his first occasion in North America and we were able to share our practice a number of times. Over dinner one fine autumn evening, it struck me how appropriate our meeting was: Sifu's four senior disciples in North America and our Si-heng from the Far East, together at last.

Returning home after dinner, I'd taken a walk along the bay. It was an evening of exceptional radiance, and near midnight the surface of the water was illumined with rich moonlight. Nearing the area where I practice each morning, it was the obvious thing to begin dancing in honor of the special circumstances that had at last closed the circle of Sifu and his dharma heirs. In the stillness of the forest edge by the shore, the chi moved like an elixir.

Early next morning Jimmy Chen, my third Tai Chi brother, now Sifu Jimmy with his own students, called with news. Sifu had died in the night and begun his journey to the Celestial Realm. Already Jimmy and Kuen were making arrangements with Sifu's family and the Taoist temple in Chinatown. There would be one last formal ceremony with our master.

Sifu was sent off in the old Chinese style: with chanting, votive and funerary offerings, the full ritual treatment. His five dharma heirs knocked their heads to the floor in full kowtow obeisance. That evening, my own students, led by Chu, a Taiwanese immigrant, began addressing me as Sifu.

As more and more of us seek to overcome the spiritual vacuum of the present age, it can be instructive to remember the model of Asia's old teaching masters and the source of their strength. Often, their gifts and talents are mistaken for mystic insight. More often than not, however, their powers derive from patience, from simple kindliness, and from diligent perseverance in a traditional wisdom path—a practice bundle known to Taoist and Buddhist traditions alike as "The Secret of the Whispered Transmission."

If Asian masters have anything to offer us in the West, it is simply themselves and their example. Mastery, whether of Tai Chi or any other spiritual practice, is more than an intellectual idea. In its proper sense—and in a way that existed in Europe and parts of North America until only twenty-five or thirty years ago—mastery is a comprehensive path for living mindfully and responsibly.

As a young immigrant to North America in the 1950s, I learned how mastery of any sort when unconnected with celebrity is so lightly valued here. My father earned his living as a stonemason. Trained in the Old Country, he worked his way through the guilds' system, eventually earning the respected title of master. On the first day of school each year, I therefore answered the teacher's critical question of "And what does your father do for a living?" with the reply, "He's a master mason." My puzzlement grew more uncomfortable each year when the new teacher invariably countered, "Do you mean a lodge member or a *bricklayer?*" and as I nodded assent to the latter, I saw this honorable but clearly diminutive title entered in my teacher's God-like ledger. Annually, I was reminded how little meaning mastery had in a culture where only higher-income professions, and the fastest routes to them, were regarded as worthy of serious merit.

In our Western egalitarian urge to banish trivial titles and honors—the baronets and marquises—inadvertently, we also lose out on much of the beauty inherent in the individual acquisition, and communal recognition, of genuine mastery—the master baker, the master plumber, the master fisher. As we discover through practices such as Tai Chi, mastery is a ripening—a "mystery" as the medieval guilds each referred to their craftwork—that matures through long years of doing, and of having done, and that goes beyond mere academic doctrine. This is the kung fu of Asia's wisdom traditions, beyond simple academies, and it is not for nothing that Taoists cherish the primal nature of the universe, of the holy Tao, as the "mystery of the uncarved block." Like the stonecutters of fifty-five centuries, they have learned that only with patient chisel and the yielding softness of the waterwheel can we truly realize the potential of making its healing spirit sing.

I bow again to these wise traditions and to my precious teachers, acknowledging their mastery and knowing that they are always with me, moving and returning again and again to the stillness.

ACKNOWLEDGMENTS

I OWE PARTICULAR THANKS TO Douglas Lau, Fred Young, and Jimmy and Jenny Chen for their long years of support, advice, translation assistance, and friendship within Sifu Ng's Tai Chi family. Special thanks also to Michael Lo, President, Kingston College, Vancouver and Toronto, for his assistance with the Tai Chi Sword sequence translation. Aloha to Matthew Lore who understood what it was about right from the beginning, and to my agents Robert Mackwood and Sally Harding. To Kuen and Hau for keeping it alive in Hong Kong, *Doh-Je*. To Norah, Vi, Betty, and Fung-I, who have stayed with it so long, a big old-fashioned hug. Alec and Shud Laeng Ma made it possible for their beloved parents Sifu and Simo Ng to be in Canada, and their children Grace, Dr. Daniel, and Edwin Ma helped Canadianize them just a little bit.

Finally, to Kwangshik, Patrick Young-Ho, and Erin Young-Ae as always, and to my clan kin, colleagues, and my students for their comments, suggestions, and ideas.

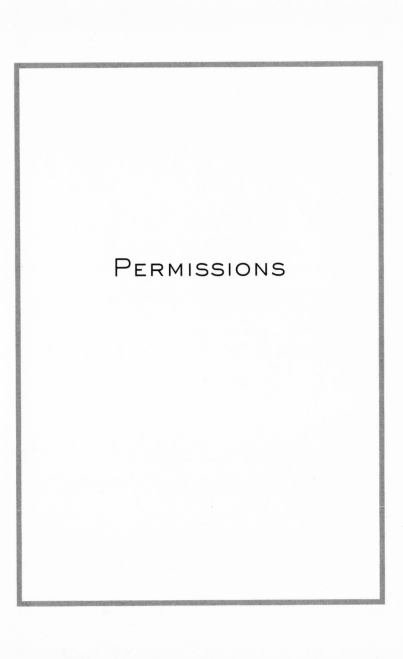

PERMISSIONS

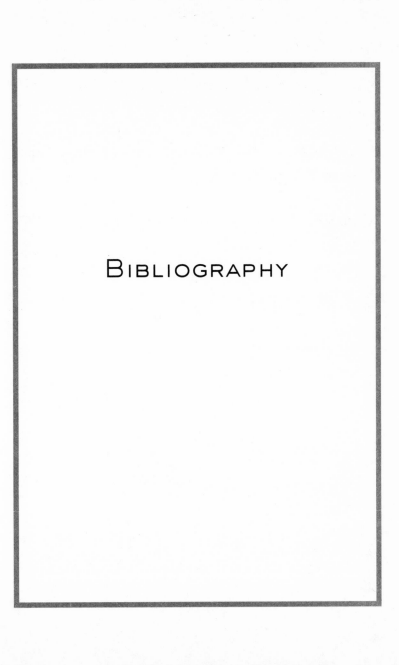

BIBLIOGRAPHY

Some helpful books through the years have included:

Aitken, Robert. *Encouraging Words: Zen Buddhist Teachings for Western Students.* New York: Pantheon, 1993. Anything by this profoundly moral American teacher is worth having.

Caesar, Julius. *The Conquest of Gaul.* Translated by Jane Gardner. London: Penguin Classics, 1951.

Capra, Fritjof. *The Tao of Physics.* Boston: Shambhala, 1975. A magnificent study.

—.*Uncommon Wisdom.* New York: Bantam, 1988. Useful.

Chang, Chung-yuan. *Creativity and Taoism: A Study of Chinese Philosophy, Art, and Poetry.* New York: Harper & Row, 1970. Excellent.

Chang, Garma, transl. *The Hundred Thousand Songs of Milarepa.* Boston: Shambhala, 2000.

Chuang-tzu. *Basic Writings.* Translated by Burton Watson. New York: Columbia University, 1964. The definitive translation of this extraordinary work.

Confucius. *The Analects.* Translated by D.C. Lau. New York: Penguin Classics, 1979. Always exquisite reading.

Dhammapada. Alhambra, Calif.: The Cunningham Press, 1955. A lovely volume of the Buddha's fundamental teachings.

Diamond Sutra. Translated by A. F. Price and Wong Mou-lam. Boston: Shambhala, 1990. Red Pine's Counterpoint edition, 2001, with extensive historical commentaries is brilliant.

Dogen, Eihei. "Treasury of the True Dharma Eye." Translated by Carl Bielefeldt. *In The Mountain Spirit,* edited by M. Tobias and H. Drasdo. Woodstock: Overlook Press, 1979.

Govinda, Anagarika Lama. *The Way of the White Clouds: A Buddhist Pilgrim in Tibet.* Berkeley: Shambhala, 1970. Brilliant Vajrayana scholarship by a beloved teacher.

H. H. the Dalai Lama of Tibet. *Ocean of Wisdom.* Toronto: McClelland & Stewart, 1989. A heart-warming compendium of guidelines for living.

—.*Stages of Meditation.* Ithaca: Snow Lion, 1991.

Lao-tzu. *Tao Te Ching of Lao Tsu.* Translated by Gia-Fu Feng and Jane English. New York: Vintage Books, 1972. A personal favorite edition that reads wonderfully well.

Loy Ching-Yuen. *The Book of the Heart: Embracing the Tao.* Translated by T. Carolan and Bella Chen. Boston: Shambhala, 1994. Poetic transliterations of Master Loy's meditations on rectifying the heart. Sifu Ng studied for many years under Loy Ching-Yuen.

—.*The Supreme Way: Inner Teachings of the Southern Mountain Tao.* Translated by T. Carolan and Du Liang. Berkeley: North Atlantic, 1997. Fine prose illuminations from Master Loy.

Maha Ghosananda. *Step by Step.* Berkeley: Parallax, 1992. Simple meditations on wisdom and compassion by Cambodia's Buddhist patriarch. A joyful little book.

Mencius. Translated by D. C. Lau. New York: Penguin Classics, 1970. A little-read masterpiece. Exquisite reading.

Merton, Thomas. *The Way of Chuang Tzu.* New York: New Directions Books, 1965. An eclectic, engaging compendium, as much about Merton as the wily Taoist master.

Musashi, Miyamoto. *A Book of Five Rings.* Translated by Victor Harris. Woodstock: Overlook Press, 1974. Essential.

Payne, David. *Confessions of a Taoist on Wall Street.* New York: Ballantine, 1984. An astounding novel of Taoist practice in exploring "the Tao within the Dow Jones."

Porter, Bill. *Road to Heaven: Encounters with Chinese Hermits.* San Francisco: Mercury, 1993. A unique book that reveals a remarkable understanding of Taoist-Buddhist lore. Dharma travel at its best.

Red Pine, trans. *The Diamond Sutra.* Washington: Counterpoint, 2001. Extraordinary range of commentary adds to a sparkling translation.

Reps, Paul. *Square Sun, Square Moon.* Rutland: Tuttle Books, 1974. Off-center vignettes. Useful.

—. *Zen Flesh, Zen Bones.* Boston: Shambhala, 1957. Irreplaceable gathering of Zen parables. Compiled with Nyogen Senzaki.

Rowland, Benjamin, Jr. *Art in East and West.* Boston: Beacon Press, 1964. Insightful discussion of aesthetics East and West. Very good.

Senzaki, Nyogen. *Like a Dream, Like a Fantasy: Zen Writings and Translations.* Translated by Eido Shimano Roshi. Tokyo: Japan Publications, Inc., 1978. Delightful *teishos,* notes, and ephemera from this seminal West Coast Zen sage.

Snyder, Gary, trans. by *The Cold Mountain Poems of Han-shan.* From "Riprap and Cold Mountain Poems," *The Evergreen Review Reader,* 1957–1967. Definitive translations in the West Coast grain.

—. *The Practice of the Wild.* San Francisco: North Point Press, 1990. A magnificent collection of essays that embrace traditional nature wisdom within contemporary environmental thought.

Stevens, John, trans. *One Robe, One Bowl: The Zen Poetry of Ryokan.* New York: Weatherhill, 1977. An excellent, definitive edition.

Sun-tzu. *The Art of War.* An indispensable Taoist masterwork. The Thomas Cleary translation (Boston, Shambhala Dragon edition) is superb; James Clavell's 1983 Delacorte edition is a surprisingly interesting abridgement.

Suzuki, D. T. *The Zen Monk's Life.* New York: The Olympia Press, 1972.

Suzuki, Shunryu. *Zen Mind, Beginner's Mind.* New York: Weatherhill, 1970. The essential introduction to Zen practice.

Thich Nhat Hanh. *Cultivating the Mind of Love.* Berkeley: Parallax, 1996. As good a book as you'll find on Zen insight training.

The Tibetan Book of the Dead. Translated by Francesca Fremantle and Chogyam Trungpa. Boston: Shambhala, 1975. Invaluable material in times of grief, or when solace is needed.

Van de Wetering, Janwillem. *The Empty Mirror.* New York: Pocket Books, 1973. An account of the author's experiences in a Kyoto Zen monastery. Useful.

—.*A Glimpse of Nothingness.* New York: Washington Square Press, 1974. The author's further adventures in an American Zen community.

Watson, Burton, trans. *Four Huts: Asian Writings on the Simple Life.* Boston: Shambhala, 1994. Exquisite renderings of four profound meditations on the rootedness of home, place, and simplicity in daily life.

Watts, Alan. *The Way of Zen.* New York: Vintage Books, 1957.

—.*The Spirit of Zen.* New York: Grove Press, 1958. Both of Watts's introductions to Zen are excellent.

Wieger, Leo. *Taoism.* Burbank: Ohara, 1976. A formidable compilation of Taoist lore, logic, history, the lot. An essential volume.

Wilhelm, Richard, trans. *I Ching, or Book of Changes.* London: Routledge and Kegan Paul, 1951. Of the many available editions, Wilhelm's is terrific and establishes the standard by which all others are measured.

About the Author

TREVOR CAROLAN regularly writes on East-West arts and culture for *Shambhala Sun, Choice, Manoa, Nguoi Viet, Kyoto Journal,* and *The Bloomsbury Review.* He has written, edited, or translated nine previous books, including (as editor) *The Colors of Heaven: Short Stories from the Pacific Rim* and (as translator) *The Supreme Way.* He lives in North Vancouver, Canada.